How To Repair
Your Scooter

Ian Paterson/Alamy

By James Manning Michels
Photography by Randy Johnson

BOONE COUNTY PUBLIC LIBRARY
BURLINGTON, KY 41005
www.bcpl.org

D1294780

Dedication

Many thanks to Bob Hedstrom. Without Bob, Neil, Stephen,
and all the rest of the gang at Scooterville in Minneapolis, Minnesota,
this book wouldn't have been the same.

First published in 2012 by Motorbooks, an imprint of MBI Publishing Company, 400 First Avenue North, Suite 300, Minneapolis, MN 55401 USA

Motorbooks titles are also available at discounts in bulk quantity for industrial or sales-promotional use. For details write to Special Sales Manager at MBI Publishing Company, 400 First Avenue North, Suite 300, Minneapolis, MN 55401 USA.

To find out more about our books, join us online at www.motorbooks.com.

ISBN-13: 978-0-7603-3986-2

Publisher: Zack Miller
Managing Editor: Jenny Miller
Editor: Darwin Holstrom
Design Manager: Brad Springer

Printed in China

On the cover: Photo by Randy Johnson

Inset: Photo by Randy Johnson

On the title page: Photo by Randy Johnson

On the back cover: Photo by Randy Johnson

About the author
James Manning Michels is a writer and editor from Minneapolis, Minnesota. Previously, he coauthored *365 Motorcycles You Must Ride*. He's an artist who's good at math. Too pop for punk, too punk for pop, when he's not riding or wrenching, he spends his time playing bass with the Minneapolis-based band 10w40.

About the photographer
Randy Johnson is a veteran Twin Cities photographer and videographer. He has worked as a photo editor at the St. Paul Pioneer Press and a photojournalism instructor at the University of Minnesota. He has contributed in a technical role to countless MBI publications for the last 20 years.

Contents

Graham Prentice/Shutterstock.com

Introduction

WHY RIDE A SCOOTER?

One reason to ride a scooter is that scooters are incredibly cheap. You can buy a new one for less than $2,000, run it for 200 miles on a couple of gallons of gas, and, by using this book, maintain it for the price of a spark plug and a few quarts of motor oil. Every now and then you'll need something else, like an air filter or some brake fluid, but scooters are to transportation as cockroaches are to living organisms—if there ever is a nuclear holocaust, both will be around afterward, and they'll both be functional. It's getting to the point where you really can't kill a scooter. But they do require at least a little preventative maintenance.

Most of all, though, scooters are fun. In some parts of the world, city streets are clogged with people riding scooters. From Rome to Jakarta, scooters are the chosen form of personal transportation—and not just because they're cheap. Walking is cheap too. Scooters are cheap, but more important, they're fun. World champion motorcycle racer Valentino Rossi honed his riding skills on a scooter tearing around the streets of his childhood home with his buddies. And, on a more utilitarian note, what's more fun: sitting in your car in rush hour traffic or zipping through idling cars and trucks on your scooter?

WHAT IS A SCOOTER?

Full disclosure: Scooters can be dangerous. Most of them have short wheelbases, steep fork angles, and small-diameter wheels. These qualities add up to twitchy machines that respond to the slightest input. Hit a bump and you'll feel it;

Scooters have always been defined by their small wheels and step-through chassis.

Traditional scooter rear end. Non traditional scooter rear-end paint job.

overcorrect your steering in a corner and you'll find yourself going somewhere you hadn't intended. They are, after all, motorized vehicles. Even a bicycle can get you into trouble. Put a motor on it and you'll have to exercise some caution. So don't ride around drunk, talking on your mobile phone while you're thinking about that cute cashier you saw at the gas station the last time you were there—two weeks ago—and you should be fine.

Scooters were never terribly popular in the United States until the twenty-first century. Then gas hit $4 a gallon for

Scooter riders come in all shapes and sizes.

continuously variable transmission using a torque converter, clutch, and a drive belt. Wheels can be anywhere from 10 inches in diameter to 16 inches, but smaller wheels are most common.

WHO CAN RIDE A SCOOTER AND WHERE CAN THEY RIDE THEM?

Anyone with a properly endorsed driver's license can ride a scooter. Not everyone who can get a properly endorsed license *should* ride them, though. If, for example, balance is an issue, or your legs don't work quite the way they should, you're better off not riding one. Same goes if you're prone to temper tantrums.

If they can reach posted minimum speeds, scooters can legally be driven on highways. Legal and practical are, of course, two different issues. It's one thing to be in freeway traffic on a scooter with a 600cc engine and 16-inch wheels; it's something entirely different to be out there on a 50cc scooter with 10-inch wheels. Even if it can get you up to 45 miles per hour (or even 50 going downhill with a tailwind), playing with cars and trucks that are traveling much faster is downright scary. So choose your battles. Yes, you might have the legal right to be out there, but it also might not be in your best interest.

the first time, and suddenly scooters were everywhere—on college campuses, in city centers. People who needed efficient transportation turned to scooters. As demand grew, so did the supply. Manufacturers started offering all kinds of scooters, from tiny 50cc machines to big 600cc bikes that, if not for their step-through design, might be confused with motorcycles. If you can't find a scooter that fits your needs and wants, you're not looking hard enough.

Which brings us to a working definition of a scooter: a small, two-wheeled vehicle with a step-through frame and a platform on which the rider rests his or her feet. Although not mandatory, most scooter engines are under the seat, and power is usually transferred to the back wheel by a

Overall, though, scooters are an incredibly efficient, and most important, fun mode of transportation—especially for urban use. They can cut through congested traffic, and once you get where you're going, you can park your scooter almost anywhere. So use some judgment and you'll find that a scooter is your best transportation option.

PROJECT PLANNING KEY

PROJECT 37
Remove Rear Turn-Signal Assembly

 Time: Given in hours or minutes

 Cost: Given on a scale of 1-4 dollar signs, with 4 dollar signs being most expensive

 Tools: Given in names of noteworthy tools (not meant to be all-inclusive)

 Parts: Given in names of noteworthy parts (not meant to be all-inclusive)

 Talent: Given on a scale of 1-5, with 5 meaning the most talent is needed

 Benefit: Given in flowing prose

This is a sample of a graphic you'll see at the beginning of each project in this book. It includes the time, tools talent, cost, parts, and, in some instances, benefits of taking on this job.

SECTION 1
BASICS

Whenever we set out to do something new, we have to start somewhere. Even though it would be more entertaining for your humble author to write a magnificent treatise on the history of the scooter, beginning with a particularly bright Cro-Magnon's discovery that an exceptionally round log would roll down a hill, such a self-indulgent digression would likely be more entertaining for the writer than the reader. Since the focus of this book is on the practical, we might as well start with the basics.

Chapter 1
Routine Maintenance vs. Repair

Keep your scooter in shape and it'll keep you moving.

ermess/Shutterstock.com

BASICS

First, we need to define "maintenance" and "repair." Maintenance work is done to stave off repair work. Repairs will always be necessary, and maintenance must be performed regularly, but the more you adhere to a regular maintenance schedule, the less frequently you'll need to repair your scooter. Most scooter owners think they'll maintain their bikes properly. Sadly, life sidetracks even the best intentions.

Every scooter comes with an owner's manual. If you don't have one, get one. They're available online, and most can be downloaded for free. You should also get a factory service manual for your scooter. It's expensive, but it will pay for itself the first time you use it. At the very least,

should a part need to be repaired, you'll be able to remove it yourself and bring it to the shop, rather than pay the shop to remove it before they fix it. Should a part simply need to be replaced, you'll be able to avoid the dealer's service bay altogether.

Anyway, look in your owner's manual. You'll find a chart detailing service procedures that should be performed at specific mileage marks. Some occur more frequently (engine oil changes) than others (replacing spark plugs). You won't notice an immediate benefit with the regular maintenance tasks, such as changing engine oil or brake fluid, until your oil loses all ability to lubricate and your crankshaft bearings freeze, or your brake fluid has absorbed so much moisture that it boils and expands and locks up your brake calipers. Tasks like replacing spark plugs or greasing chassis points are easy to quantify: Your engine won't misfire anymore and your chassis won't squeak as you bounce down the road. Remember, evidence of application has nothing to do with importance of application. All maintenance items must be performed as scheduled if you want to avoid as much repair work as you can.

Which brings us to the definition of repair work. Scooters have become pretty close to bulletproof, especially if they're maintained properly. But scooters are made up of mechanical objects and depend on moving parts—and they contain hazardous liquids, some of which can burst into flames. Combustion chambers are subject to copious amounts of pressure; crankshafts spin around in complete circumferences thousands of times every minute; valves open and close in a fraction of a second—and that's just the engine. Wheels spin on their bearings, suspension dampers are in constant motion, and turn signals are made to flash. Your scooter is a complex system of mechanical components working in harmony, asked to perform every time you turn the ignition key to "On" and hit the starter button.

All components will eventually fail, due to manufacturing defects or plain old wear and tear. Piston rings lose their ability to seal; shock absorbers lose their ability to damp suspension movement; turn-signal bulb filaments burn through. Keeping engine oil fresh can minimize piston-ring replacement. Turn-signal bulb replacement can only be put off by not using your turn signals—certainly not a recommended practice. The point of all this? Regular maintenance will keep the serious stuff at bay, but there are going to be repairs eventually.

So what's maintenance and what's repair work? Maintenance is like preventative medicine. Exercise regularly and eat properly, and your chances of becoming ill or injured are considerably reduced. You still might fall off, say, a scooter and break your arm, but your ability to recover quickly is much better. In the same vein, change your scooter's engine coolant regularly, and the cooling system itself stands a much better chance of maintaining pressure, vital to proper operation. Continually top off the reservoir with tap water, and your radiator will become calcified and corroded, eventually springing pinhole leaks. Changing coolant is maintenance; changing radiators is repair work.

FLUIDS

Your scooter relies on a number of fluids. Some lubricate, some transfer heat, some are pushed through passageways, either to move something on the other end or to absorb energy through being pushed. Whatever their job, fluids break down over time and must be replaced. Between replacements, they leak, burn away, or otherwise disappear, and reservoirs must be topped off. Pay close attention to your scooter's fluid levels and conditions.

LUBRICANTS

First up are lubricants. As discussed above, engine lubricant (oil) performance is vital. Equally important is the lubricant in the transmission's final-drive box. This is where engine power actually turns the rear wheel. The engine's crankshaft turns the variator, the variator turns the drive belt, the drive belt turns the clutch, and the clutch shaft turns a series of helical reduction gears in the drive box that end up turning the rear wheel axle. These reduction gears operate in an oil bath. Should the drive box oil level get too low, the viscous film protecting the gear teeth becomes insufficient or even nonexistent. Metal bearing directly on metal wears quickly. Moreover, metal bearing on metal gets extremely hot. When this happens to gears, teeth chip and break off. At best, your scooter's drive box will whine loudly. At worst, riding your scooter with a dry gearbox could cause the final drive to seize up completely.

Oils are graded according to viscosity. Viscosity is, basically, a measure of tensile strength. The higher the number, the greater the viscosity. For example, 90-weight gearbox oil is thicker than 30-weight engine oil and has greater tensile strength. Greater tensile strength is a good thing. On the other hand, thicker fluid has a harder time getting through narrow passageways, like oil journals in a four-stroke engine. Plus, thicker oil takes longer to heat up, compounding the narrow-passageway flowing problem. So don't fill your engine's oil reservoir, called the oil sump, with gearbox oil.

Engine oils come in a variety of viscosity appellations. While straight-weight oil is available, such as 30-weight, most engine oils have viscosities designated by two numbers, like 5W30 or 20W50. The first number is the viscosity as tested at cold temperatures (the "W" in the appellation stands for Winter). The second is the viscosity as tested at high temperatures. Straight-weight oil has only been tested at high temperatures.

Since thinner-viscosity oil flows better when cold, it gives less dry running time after an engine is first started. In other words, if you have 5W30 oil in your scooter, metal parts will be rubbing against each other unprotected for a certain amount of time when you fire up your engine each morning. If you're using straight 30-weight, that unprotected rubbing time will be much longer, and your engine will wear out much faster. Most engine wear occurs in the first five minutes of running time after a cold start; oil designed for use when cold minimizes this damage dramatically.

Check your owner's manual. It will have a chart designating which oil viscosities should be used in what temperature ranges. Follow the suggestions in that chart. And, just as important, change oils at the mileage or time intervals suggested in the service-procedures chart. Oil viscosity breaks down over time. Old oil loses its ability to provide a protective film. Therefore, old oil is just this side of useless.

In addition to differences in viscosity, engine oils are also available in a variety of chemical formulas. Without getting into too much depth, the choices are carbon-based, synthetic, or a combination of the two. Carbon-based oils are less expensive; semi-synthetics are more expensive; full synthetics are most expensive. As with most things, you get what you pay for. Fully synthetic oils provide the best protection, for the longest time.

It's quite possible that, if you change your scooter's oil often enough, before the viscosity begins to break down, you'll notice no difference between carbon-based and fully synthetic oil. On the other hand, engines that used only fully synthetic oil, changed regularly, have been torn apart after hundreds of thousands of miles of use to demonstrate parts that show very, very little wear. Factor in the added cost of more frequent oil changes with carbon-based products, and synthetic seems the clear choice. At least go for a semi-synthetic.

COOLANT

Not all scooter engines are liquid cooled, but if yours is, next on the list of fluids to monitor is engine coolant (sometimes called anti-freeze). Of course, it must be maintained at the proper level in the reservoir. You can top up the reservoir with plain water (never use tap water, only distilled water) in an emergency, but it's best to use a 50/50 mix of water and coolant. When using your scooter in extremely cold weather, the mix ratio might need to be altered to prevent the coolant mix from freezing and rupturing hoses or cracking the engine block.

Every so often (check your owner's manual for recommended intervals), the entire engine cooling system must be flushed and refilled. First, over time, coolant loses its ability to absorb heat from the engine and transfer it to the radiator for dissipation. Second, old coolant can acquire an electrical charge, a process called electrolysis. Third, engine coolant contains chemicals that not only conduct heat, but they lubricate parts and prevent corrosion. These chemicals lose their usefulness as time passes on. So old engine coolant not only loses its ability to do its job, it becomes downright harmful.

Remember, every time you start your scooter's engine, its coolant mixture goes from ambient temperature to hundreds of degrees Fahrenheit. Then, after you shut the engine off, it returns to ambient temperature. How many heat cycles has your scooter's engine coolant gone through? Probably way more than you can count. This is why it's important to drain, flush, and fill your scooter's engine cooling system at the intervals listed in your owner's manual.

BRAKES

If your scooter has fluid reservoirs on the handlebar levers, it has hydraulic brakes. The system is simple: The lever pushes a piston, which pushes hydraulic fluid, in this case, brake

If there's a reservoir on the handlebars, your scooter has a hydraulic brake. Hydraulic brakes are more powerful and less prone to failure than cable-operated brakes. As the name *hydraulic* implies, they rely on fluid in order to operate. The level of fluid in the reservoir must be maintained; otherwise the brake won't work.

fluid, through a line to force another piston to move. With disc brakes, the fluid pushes a piston in the brake caliper, forcing the brake pads to clamp onto the brake disc. In drum brakes, the fluid pushes the brake shoes outward against the inside of the brake drum. Whether disc or drum brakes, friction caused by applying the pads or shoes against the disc or drum stops the wheel from turning. Disc brakes are more effective; drum brakes are more forgiving. Which is a polite way of saying they don't work as well.

Brake fluid is hygroscopic, which means it absorbs water. If left out and exposed to the air, even new brake fluid will absorb moisture and be rendered useless. So make sure to only use fresh brake fluid from a sealed container when topping off or flushing and filling your scooter's brake systems. And, since old brake fluid eventually breaks down, not to mention absorbs moisture, be sure to change brake fluid as recommended by your owner's manual. At best, old fluid will give your brakes a spongy feel. At worst, the heat created by the friction of the stopping process will be transferred to the old brake fluid, causing the absorbed moisture to expand. If this happens, it will force the caliper piston out, clamping the brake pads against the disc—without you even touching the brake lever on the handlebars. You'll be able to get going again by releasing the hydraulic pressure through the bleeder valve on the caliper, assuming you have the proper wrench and the unannounced application of your brakes didn't cause you to crash.

Although they're not fluids, this is a good time to briefly discuss brake pads and shoes. As mentioned above, brakes employ friction. Friction causes heat, and it also causes wear. Pads and shoes are designed so that, each time they're applied, a small amount of them rubs away. This is why brakes get so dusty and dirty. Eventually, the abrasive surfaces wear away completely, leaving only the metal backing to be applied to the disc or drum, causing it to get severely scored. Don't let

Two wheels, handlebars, and a seat are traits scooters share with motorcycles. And now monoshock rear suspensions.

this happen. Replacing brake pads and shoes is easy; replacing discs and drums is much more involved. Pad and shoe wear can be monitored visually. Do it. If you forget, and your brakes start making a metallic rubbing sound, stop riding immediately and replace your pads or shoes.

SUSPENSION

Your suspension system uses dampers to minimize oscillation after you hit a bump. These dampers employ hydraulics to absorb the energy retained in the spring after it's made to move, either in compression or extension. The hydraulic fluid in your shocks and forks needs to be maintained at the proper level. It also needs to be changed every so often. Shocks might be problematic; normally they just get replaced when the fluid wears out (noticeable by the way your scooter keeps bouncing after it hits a bump). Forks, on the other hand, are more usually able to have their fluid changed. Check your scooter's service manual.

FILTERS

Dirt is your scooter's enemy. Dirt causes wear, dirt builds up and impedes flow. Sadly, dirt is everywhere. Impurities can be washed off the exterior of your scooter easily enough, but once a grain of sand gets into your crankshaft bearing, or a chunk of vegetation gets sucked into your carburetor, it's just a matter of time before the bearing fails or the carb gets clogged. So your scooter's internals need to be protected. This is where filters come in.

Oil

Your scooter's engine oil resides in the oil sump. From there, it is pumped through passageways, called journals, to various places throughout the engine, where it bathes bushings, bearings, and other moving parts, covering them

in a protective film. Impurities in the oil will wear out these parts. Impurities can also plug up the journals, leaving the parts completely unprotected.

Oil is continually pumped through the journals, bathing parts and returning to the sump. On the way back to the sump, the oil is routed through the oil filter, where any impurities the oil gathered in its travels are removed before it gets back to the sump. Over time, the filter collects a lot of stuff, impeding oil flow. Changing the oil filter ensures a constant supply of fresh oil will always bathe your engine's internals.

Air

Your scooter sucks an incredible amount of air into the carburetor. About 14 times as much air goes through

Your scooter's air filter is the only thing keeping the engine from sucking up dirt, sand, butterflies, and whatever else is floating around. Air travels through the intake manifold at very high speeds. Get some crud in the airflow, and it's like sandblasting all the plastic, aluminum, and brass passageways in the fuel intake system.

11

A well-worn tire is a badge of honor. It means you've been riding your scooter hard. Of course, "well-worn" means the tire's been worn from side to side from leaning the scooter into turns, not simply left on until the cords start showing. That would just be a worn-out tire. This is a well-worn tire. Its owner has been riding his scooter hard.

the carb as does fuel. Inside the carb are tiny passageways and nozzles, each of which could become plugged by dirt. Not only that, the air/fuel mixture is pulled at a high rate of speed through the carb and intake ports, past the valves, and into the combustion chamber. Dirt in the mixture will bounce off all the alloy and plastic surfaces along the way. After a while, these surfaces will become deformed, affecting flow.

It is important to keep your scooter's air filter clean. Some air filters can only be replaced; others can be cleaned periodically before they need to be replaced. Check your owner's manual for service intervals. If you ride in dustier than normal conditions, clean your scooter's air filter more frequently than the owner's manual recommends.

Fuel

This is the filter most often neglected. Some scooters don't even come with a fuel filter. If yours didn't, install one. Even if gas were to come out of the pump clean (it doesn't), stuff gets inside the tank, sticks to the walls, then gets washed away by the sloshing gas. Sometimes the tank walls themselves corrode, and impurities get into the gas that way. As discussed above in the air filter section, dirt in the air/fuel mix causes a multitude of problems.

As with all filters, over time, fuel filters get filled with crud and start impeding the flow of gas to the carb. Some fuel filters can be cleaned; others must be replaced. Either way, don't neglect your scooter's fuel filter.

SPARK PLUGS AND SPARK-PLUG WIRES

Since your scooter probably has an electronic ignition, you don't have to worry about adjusting the timing. In fact, the

only maintenance you'll be able to perform on the ignition is changing the plugs at the intervals recommended in your owner's manual. Occasionally you'll need to replace the high-tension lead going from the ignition module to the spark plug, but only if it starts leaking current.

Be sure to use the proper replacement plug. Spark plugs come in a variety of types and sizes. Thread size, reach, and temperature range are just a few of the attributes that differ from one plug to the next. Again, check your owner's manual.

FUSES

Sometimes something on your scooter just won't work. Maybe the starter motor doesn't engage; maybe the headlight doesn't come on. If you suspect an electrical problem, the first thing to check is the fuse that regulates the circuit. Fuses are located in a number of places on your scooter. Fusebox locations are noted in the owner's manual.

BATTERY

Your scooter has a 12-volt electrical system. Everything runs off the battery, which is continually charged by the alternator. If the alternator doesn't put out about 14 amps, the battery won't charge, and the continued draw from operating your scooter's electrical system will run the battery down until it finally won't have enough electricity stored to power your scooter.

More often, though, the problem is with battery maintenance. If your scooter sits unused for long periods of time, the battery will run down and need to be charged. So if you know you're not going to use your scooter for a while, take the battery out and put it on a trickle charger.

If you don't have a trickle charger, at least put the battery on a conventional charger (no more than 2 amps charging capability) every few weeks.

It's also a good idea to keep your battery's terminals clean. Disconnect the battery and thoroughly clean the terminals and cable ends using a wire brush and baking soda solution or a purposely developed battery terminal cleaner. The idea is to remove all the corrosion from the contact points of the terminal and cable ends. Corrosion will prevent the charge from transmitting between the battery to the cable. You can even get battery terminal protector to spray on the clean connections after the cable has been reattached.

Most batteries sold today are sealed, so there's no maintenance to be done with respect to battery acid. If you have an unsealed battery, however, it is important to monitor the fluid level inside. Simply remove the stoppers for each of the six cells and make a visual check. If you can see the battery plates, the fluid level is too low, and the plates can start to corrode. Top up cells as necessary with distilled water. Warning: Never use tap water for this.

One important note: Be very careful not to bridge the positive and negative terminals, or to bridge the positive terminal and any ground (metal part of your scooter). The latter usually happens when you are disconnecting the positive cable. So, when disconnecting the cables, disconnect the negative cable first. This opens the electrical circuit, removing power from everything. If you disconnect the positive cable first, power surges can occur if the cable end is removed and then momentarily regains contact with the battery terminal. The downside is that you must be extra cautious, after disconnecting the negative cable, not to let the wrench you're using to disconnect the positive cable make contact with anything metal. Might as well just say don't let it make contact with anything, just to be safe.

And, of course, always make sure that positive cables, whether from the scooter's electrical system or from the battery charger, connect to the positive terminal on the battery, and that the negative cables always connect to the negative terminal. Double check. Then check again. A moment's mistake here can cost hundreds of dollars.

TIRES

Your scooter's tires are your interface with the road, the only physical contact point between the two of you. A good interface is so unnoticeable you don't even think about it. A bad interface can leave both you and your scooter badly damaged. Make sure to inspect your tires frequently.

First, of course, make sure your tires are properly inflated. Refer to your owner's manual for proper inflation levels for the way you'll be using your scooter. There is also an inflation figure molded into the side of each tire itself—*do not inflate either tire to this level*. This is the maximum pressure that the tire is designed for, not the suggested running pressure. There

are any number of ways your scooter's tires can blow out if they're inflated to the pressure level molded onto the tire wall.

Once inflated properly, checking each tire's pressure is vitally important, even if you just squeeze it with your hand every time you go for a ride to get a feel for how much air's in there. But use an air-pressure gauge regularly—both to get an accurate numerical analysis and to calibrate your hand.

If your scooter wallows around and feels mushy through turns, it's a good bet your tire pressure is too low. Hit a bump with underinflated tires, and you'll dent your rim, blow out the tire, or both. If your scooter skitters around corners as though it's nervous, or you can feel everything you roll over, most likely your tire pressure is too high.

Be sure to have an air source handy when you check tire pressure. If your tires are underinflated, the need is obvious. But even if you're trying to take air out of overinflated tires, you might overshoot and need to add some back. Also, pressure should be checked when the tires are cold, before you've ridden on them. As your scooter rolls down the road, the carcass of each tire flexes. This repeated flexing action creates heat, and, as you remember from high-school physics class, heat and pressure are directly linked—as one increases, so does the other. So check your tires when they're cold. If you have to ride someplace in order to get access to compressed air, check tire pressures again when you get there and figure the difference into your target pressures.

And be sure to keep track of tire wear. Some wear is obvious. When the tread blocks wear away and your tires are bald—or, worse, the cords are showing—you should get new tires. Less obvious, though, is the effect of all the flexing referred to above. Each time the sidewall flexes, it becomes weaker and will fail eventually. Sometimes this wear can be seen in the form of tiny cracks in the rubber. But if your tires' lives can be measured in years, you should probably go ahead and replace them even if you can't see any cracks.

Follow the maintenance schedule in your scooter owner's manual, and you'll have a comfortable, reliable ride.

PROJECT 1
Remove, Check, and Replace Spark Plug

 Time: 1 hour

 Tools: Screwdriver; spark-plug wrench; torque wrench and spark-plug socket

 Talent: 2

 Cost: $

 Parts: Spark plug; anti-seize compound

 Benefit: A running engine; knowledge of how well your engine is running; knowledge of whether the air/fuel mixture is too rich, too lean, or just right

1 Locate the spark plug. See the owner's manual. Remove body panels as necessary to expose the plug. (See chapter 13.) Some scooters have special access panels; others require removal of the entire body panel. Even if your scooter has an access panel, sometimes it's easier to just go ahead and take off the whole body panel because that gives you more unfettered access. *Inset:* Remove the spark-plug cap. Don't yank on the wire itself or you'll just separate it from the spark-plug cap. Grasp the plug cap itself firmly and pull it straight back from the plug.

2

Spark-plug sockets come in a variety of sizes. Make sure you have the right one for your scooter's spark plug. A deep-wall socket of the proper size can also be used, but they're not as efficient, especially when it's time to reinstall the plug. Spark-plug sockets have rubber inserts that follow the shape of the plug, allowing it to nestle inside the socket. When reinstalling the plug, this insert holds the plug in the socket more firmly, so you can more easily align the threads when first screwing in the plug. Cross-threading threads in the cylinder head is a common mistake and can be expensive to repair. It's the threads in the aluminum cylinder head that will strip, not the steel threads on the spark plug. Using the proper spark-plug socket, unscrew the spark plug and remove it.

3

Inspect the plug. If there's flat black residue, the engine is running too rich. If there's white residue, the engine is running too hot and probably lean. Gray or light tan residue indicates an engine that's running well. Clean the plug with electrical contact cleaner and a wire brush. Inspect the gap between the center and side electrodes with a gap gauge as shown here. Adjust if necessary (consult the owner's manual for specifications). If the plug has been used for more than 20,000 miles or two years, don't bother checking, cleaning, or adjusting the plug. Just replace it with a new one.

4

Apply anti-seize compound to the plug threads.

5

Reinstall the plug. Be careful not to cross-thread. Tighten to finger tight first.

6

Use a torque wrench to tighten to proper torque. Consult the owner's manual for torque specifications. Do not over tighten. *Inset:* Reinstall the spark-plug cap. Reinstall the access or body panels as necessary.

PROJECT 2
Remove, Clean, and Replace Air Filter

 Time: 1 hour

 Tools: Screwdriver; compressed air; plastic bag

 Talent: 2

 Cost: $

 Parts: Air filter (if it is being replaced); air filter oil

Benefit: A better-breathing fuel intake system; less grit clogging up carburetor orifi or fuel-injector nozzles

1 Locate the air-filter assembly. Consult the scooter owner's or service manual.

2

Remove the air-filter housing cover retaining screws.

3

Pull off the air-filter housing cover.

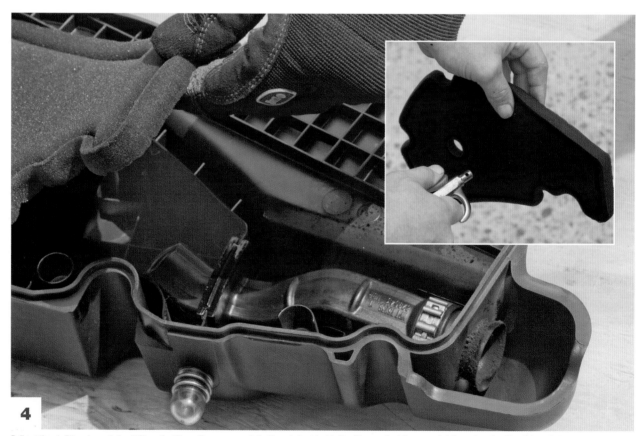

4

Pull out the air-filter element. *Inset:* Clean the filter with compressed air. Blow air from inside the filter, against the normal airflow when the filter is installed.

5

Pour air-filter oil onto the filter. Don't overdo it. You don't need to cover the entire filter, but do try to get some oil on all sides of any interruptions in the filter, such as screw holes.

6

Put the filter in an appropriately sized plastic bag and squeeze the bag from the outside. Do not wring the life out of the air filter, but squeeze it gently. Work air-filter oil into air filter completely.

7

Remove the air filter from bag and gently squeeze it to remove excess oil (do not wring out the filter or it will begin to break down). Reinstall the filter into the air-filter housing. Replace the air-filter housing cover and retaining screws.

PROJECT 3
Check Tire Air Pressure

 Time: 10 minutes

 Tools: Air-pressure gauge; compressed air or tire pump

 Talent: 1

 Cost: None

 Parts: None

 Benefit: A better-handling scooter; longer tire life

1 Remove the valve-stem cap.

2

Use an air-pressure gauge to check the tire's air pressure. Be quick and sure when putting the air-pressure gauge's chuck onto the valve stem. The less air you let out when putting the chuck onto or taking it off of the valve stem, the more accurate your reading will be. If you get too sloppy, you can let out whole pounds of air pressure. Air pressure gauges come in a variety of types. Some are simple, relying on air pressure to push a graduated stick out of a pen-shaped housing; others are more complex, using a hose that attaches the valve stem to a digital or analog gauge. Prices range from a couple of dollars to a couple of hundred dollars. Whatever type you get, take it somewhere and check it against a calibrated gauge. Don't worry if yours reads differently, just remember what the difference is. Then simply add or subtract the difference whenever you use your gauge. It's a linear system, so differences won't be multiplied as readings get higher.

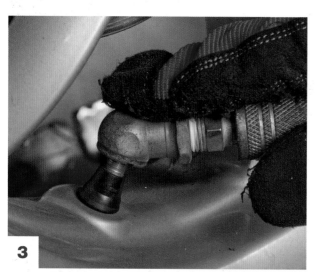

3

If the reading is too high, let out some air and recheck. Repeat until the reading is correct. If the reading is too low, add compressed air and recheck. Repeat until the reading is correct. It's helpful to count while air escapes or enters the tire. After a while, you'll get to know just how long it takes to let a pound of air out or put a pound in. Also, the suggested tire pressures in your scooter owner's manual are for cold tires. Remember that tires heat up as they roll down the road, which means the air inside them also heats up. Hot air expands, increasing its pressure. So it's best to check tire air pressure when the tires are cold, before they've taken you anywhere. If you have to check pressure when the tires are warm, be aware that the readings will be higher. Don't adjust those pressures to meet the specified pressure in the owner's manual. It's more important that front and back tire pressures match than meet specification in this instance.

4 Replace the cap.

PROJECT 4
Change Gearbox Oil

 Time: 1 hour

 Tools: Wrench; torque wrench and socket; oil drain pan; funnel or squeeze bottle; oily rag and smoldering ashes

 Talent: 1

 Cost: $

 Parts: Gear oil; crush-washer for drain plug

Benefit: Longer gearbox life

1

The gearbox oil should be changed every 4,000 miles or every two years, whichever comes first. Consult your owner's manual or your scooter's service manual to determine the amount of gearbox oil you'll need to put back into the gearbox after you've drained the old oil. There also might be a sticker on the gearbox, or the capacity could be stamped onto the gearbox housing itself. First, locate the gearbox fill plug. *Inset:* Clean the gearbox case, especially around the filler and drain holes. Remove the fill plug. Inspect the O-ring. Don't lose it. Thoroughly clean the fill plug, O-ring, and gearbox case around the fill hole.

2

Locate the gearbox drain plug.

3

Put a suitably sized drain pan under the drain plug. Using the properly sized wrench, loosen the drain plug until it can be unscrewed with your fingers.

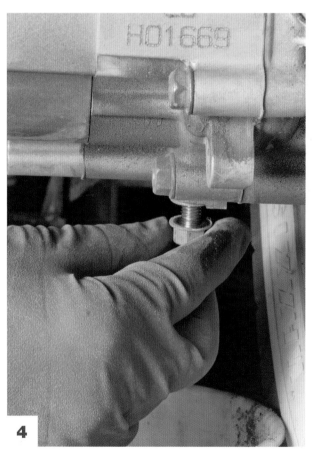

4

Continue loosening the drain plug with your fingers until only the last few threads are engaged. Then grasp the plug firmly and push it in against its threads and continue unscrewing. The idea is to minimize the amount of oil that comes out. After the threads are completely disengaged, seat the plug in the drain hole for a moment, gather yourself, then pull the plug out and away in one decisive motion. Try to keep hold of the plug when it does come out, otherwise you'll have to drag your fingers through the oil in the drain pan. Be careful not to lose the washer.

5

Let oil to drain into drain pan. Gearbox oil is thick. Even when it seems to just be trickling out, it could go on like that for a while. Allow enough time for all the oil to drain.

6

There isn't an enormous quantity of oil in the gearbox; all the more reason to change it regularly. If there's a lot of sludge in the drain pan, you waited too long.

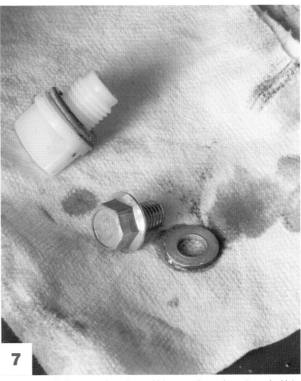

7

Drain plugs typically use crush washers, which means the washer gets crushed into position when the drain plug is torqued into place. If your scooter uses a crush washer, it must be replaced every time the drain plug is loosened. If your scooter doesn't use a crush washer, clean and inspect the drain-plug washer and replace if necessary.

8

With the proper washer in place, reinstall drain plug. Screw it in until it is finger tight.

9

Tighten with a torque wrench to the proper torque. The torque value is listed in your scooter owner's or service manual.

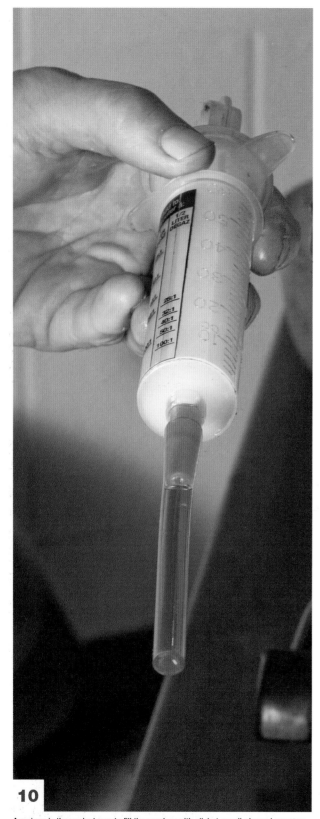

10

A syringe is the easiest way to fill the gearbox with oil, but a well-cleaned squeeze bottle, like a ketchup or shampoo bottle, also works. A bottle of oil and a funnel will suffice, but gearbox fill openings are usually hard to access, so a container that offers you the ability to control flow is best.

11

Check your scooter owner's or service manual to determine how much oil your scooter's gearbox holds. Fill a measuring device with the proper amount of oil.

12

Suck the measured amount of oil into the syringe or pour it into a squeeze bottle.

13 Put the oil into the gearbox.

14 Wipe off any excess oil from the filler opening.

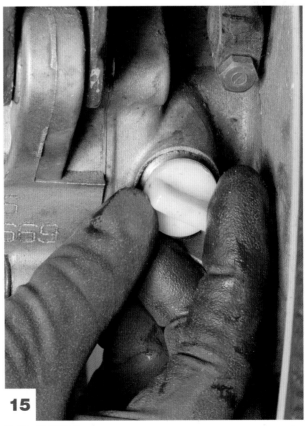

15 Replace the filler cap.

25

SECTION 2
ENGINE AND TRANSMISSION

The reason they're called "motor scooters" is that they have motors. These remarkable devices allow riders to power their way around town and over the Swiss Alps. But they also require much maintenance and repair. This can seem a daunting task, but don't despair—the goal of this book is to make the repair and maintenance of the engine and transmission in your scooter less daunting.

Engine Troubleshooting Guide

PROBLEM	PROBABLE CAUSES	ACTION TO REPAIR
Kick starter doesn't turn over engine	Broken kick-start lever Faulty starter gear	Replace kick-start lever Replace starter gear
Starter motor doesn't turn	No power to starter	Check fuse Check/replace battery Check/replace starter relay Check/replace ignition key switch Check/replace starter switch Check/repair/replace wiring harness Check/replace kill switch Check/replace oil warning light diode
Power to starter, but starter doesn't turn	Faulty starter	Check/replace starter motor
Starter turns, but engine doesn't turn over	Starter doesn't engage	Check/replace starter pinion-gear assembly Check/replace starter clutch Check/replace starter gear
Starter engages, but engine is frozen	Seized piston	Check/replace piston/rings
Starter engages and engine turns over but won't start	Low or no compression	Compression test Retorque spark plug Retorque cylinder head Adjust valves Check piston/cylinder tolerances Replace piston/rings/cylinder Replace cylinder head gasket Replace warped cylinder head
	Weak or no spark	Check spark strength at plug Check fuse Check/replace ignition key switch Check/repair/replace wiring harness Check/charge/replace battery Check/replace alternator Check plug type/adjust gap Check HT plug wire connection/replace HT wire Check/replace ECU Check/replace HT/source/pickup coils
	No fuel	Check fuel level in tank Check/replace gas line Clean/replace fuel filter Clean/replace carburetor
	Faulty carburetion	Check/adjust throttle cable Check/adjust/repair/replace choke Check/adjust idle-air (pilot) screw Clean/replace air filter/check for leaks Check intake manifold for leaks/replace gaskets Drain/refill gas tank Check/adjust carburetor float level Clean/replace carburetor

PROBLEM	PROBABLE CAUSES	ACTION TO REPAIR
Engine starts then stalls	Low or no compression	Compression test
		Retorque spark plug
		Adjust valves
		Retorque cylinder head
		Replace cylinder-head gasket
		Replace warped cylinder head
		Check piston/cylinder tolerances
		Replace piston/rings/cylinder
	Faulty ignition	Check fuse
		Check spark strength at plug
		Check/adjust ignition timing
		Check/replace ECU
		Check/replace HT/source/pickup coils
		Check/repair/replace wiring harness
	Faulty carburetion	Check/adjust throttle cable
		Check/adjust/repair/replace choke
		Check/adjust idle-air (pilot) screw
		Clean/replace air filter/check for leaks
		Check intake manifold for leaks/replace gaskets
		Drain/refill gas tank
		Check/adjust carburetor float level
		Clean/replace carburetor
Engine runs poorly at low rpm	Low compression	Compression test
		Retorque spark plug
		Retorque cylinder head
		Adjust valves
		Check piston/cylinder tolerances
		Replace piston/rings/cylinder
		Replace cylinder head gasket
		Replace warped cylinder head
	Weak spark	Check spark strength at plug
		Check/charge/replace battery
		Check/replace alternator
		Check plug type/adjust gap
		Check HT plug wire connection/replace
		Check/adjust ignition timing
		Check/replace ECU
		Check/replace HT/source/pickup coils
	Faulty carburetion	Check/adjust throttle cable
		Check/adjust/repair/replace choke
		Check/adjust idle-air (pilot) screw
		Check/adjust carburetor float level
		Clean/replace carburetor
	Intake air leak	Clean/replace air filter/check for leaks
		Check intake manifold for leaks/replace gaskets
	Contaminated fuel	Drain/refill fuel tank
Engine idles roughly	Faulty ignition timing	Check spark strength at plug
		Check/adjust ignition timing
		Check/replace ECU
		Check/replace HT/source/pickup coils
	Faulty carburetion	Check/adjust/repair/replace choke
		Check/adjust idle-air (pilot) screw
		Clean/replace carburetor
		Check/replace fuel filter

PROBLEM	PROBABLE CAUSES	ACTION TO REPAIR
	Intake air leak	Clean/replace air filter/check for leaks Check intake manifold for leaks/replace gaskets
	Contaminated fuel	Drain/refill fuel tank
Engine accelerates poorly	Ignition timing not advancing	Check/replace ECU Check/replace HT/source/pickup coils
	Carburetor leaking or dirty	Clean/replace carb
	Faulty choke	Check/replace choke
	Wrong viscosity engine oil	Change oil
	Brakes dragging	Adjust cables Rebuild calipers Check/replace discs Adjust shoes Check/replace shoes
	Clutch slipping	Check/repair/replace clutch
	Faulty torque converter	Check/repair/replace torque converter
	Worn drive belt	Check/replace drive belt
Engine runs poorly at high rpm	Low compression	Compression test Retorque spark plug Retorque cylinder head Adjust valves Check piston/cylinder tolerances Replace piston/rings/cylinder Replace cylinder head gasket Replace warped cylinder head
	Weak spark	Check spark strength at plug Check/charge/replace battery Check/replace alternator Check plug type/adjust gap Check HT plug wire connection/replace Check/replace HT/source/pickup coils
	Faulty ignition timing	Check/adjust ignition timing Check/replace ECU
	Ignition timing not advancing	Check/replace ECU Check/replace HT/source/pickup coils
	Throttle not opening fully	Adjust throttle cable
	Faulty carburetion	Check/adjust/repair/replace choke Clean/replace carburetor Check/replace fuel filter
	Intake air leak	Clean/replace air filter/check for leaks Check intake manifold for leaks/replace gaskets
	Brakes dragging	Adjust cables Rebuild calipers Check/replace discs Adjust shoes Check/replace drums

PROBLEM	PROBABLE CAUSES	ACTION TO REPAIR
	Clutch slipping	Check/repair/replace clutch
	Faulty torque converter	Check/repair/replace torque converter
	Worn drive belt	Check/replace drive belt
Engine overheats	Faulty liquid-cooling system	Check/flush/refill cooling system Replace leaky/clogged hoses Check/replace thermostat Check/replace coolant pump Check/clean/replace cooling fan Check/replace fan motor/temperature sensor Check/replace fan motor switch Check/replace radiator
	Faulty air-cooling system	Check/clean fan ducts and cowling Check/replace fan
	Faulty cylinder-head gasket	Check/replace gasket
	Compression too high	Check cylinder head gasket thickness Retorque cylinder head Decarbonize cylinder head
	Exhaust valve too tight	Adjust valves
	Faulty ignition timing	Check spark strength at plug Check/adjust ignition timing Check/replace ECU Check/replace HT/source/pickup coils
	Faulty carburetion	Clean/replace air filter/check for leaks Check intake manifold for leaks/replace gaskets Check/adjust carburetor float level Clean/replace carburetor
	Inadequate engine lubrication	Check oil level and type Check/adjust oil pump cable
	Drivetrain making engine work too hard	Check/repair/replace clutch Check/repair/replace torque converter Check/replace drive belt
	Brakes making engine work too hard	Adjust cables Rebuild calipers Check/replace discs Adjust shoes Check/replace drums
Engine knocks or pings	Compression too high	Decarbonize cylinder head
	Poor-quality fuel	Drain fuel tank
	Faulty carburetion	Rebuild carb
	Intake air leak	Clean/replace air filter/check for leaks Check intake manifold for leaks/replace gaskets
Engine piston slap or rattle	Worn piston/rings/cylinder	Rebuild pistons/rings/cylinder
Engine valve noise	Valves too loose	Adjust valves

PROBLEM	PROBABLE CAUSES	ACTION TO REPAIR
Excessive exhaust noise	Exhaust header gasket leak	Replace exhaust header gasket
	Loose exhaust fittings	Retorque header, main pipe, catalytic converter, and muffler connections
Engine makes excessive white exhaust smoke	Oil getting into combustion chamber	Replace piston oil ring Rebore cylinder/install oversize piston Replace valve guides Replace valve oil seals
Engine makes excessive white/blue smoke	Excessive oil in combustion chamber	Check/adjust oil pump cable Check/replace oil pump Clean oil deposits in exhaust system (Just ride it)
Engine makes excessive black smoke	Air/fuel mixture too rich	Clean/replace air filter Check/adjust carb floats Check/clean/replace carb needle valve and seat Rebuild/rejet carb Adjust/replace choke
Engine makes excessive brown smoke	Air/fuel mixture too lean	Check air filter housing for leaks Check intake manifold for leaks
	Faulty ignition timing	Check/adjust ignition timing Check/replace ECU

Transmission Troubleshooting Guide

PROBLEM	PROBABLE CAUSES	ACTION TO REPAIR
No drive to rear wheel	Broken drive belt Faulty clutch Faulty torque converter	Check/replace drive belt Check/repair/replace clutch Check/repair/replace torque converter
Poor drive to rear wheel	Worn drive belt Dirty/worn torque converter pulleys Weak or broken driven-pulley spring Faulty clutch Faulty torque converter	Check/replace drive belt Clean/replace pulleys Check/replace driven pulley spring Check/repair/replace clutch Check/repair/replace torque converter
Excessive noise or vibration at all speeds	Faulty gearbox Faulty clutch Faulty torque converter	Check/rebuild/replace gearbox Check/repair/rebuild clutch Check/repair/replace torque converter
Excessive noise or vibration at specific speeds	Loose torque converter pulley nut Bent clutch shaft	Check/retorque torque converter pulley nuts Check/replace clutch shaft
Clutch doesn't disengage completely	Weak or broken clutch springs Engine idle speed too high	Check/repair/replace clutch Adjust idle

Chapter 2
Four-Stroke Engine

Air-quality issues are causing big changes in scooter engines. Two-stroke engines were once the staple, but four-stroke engines are taking over. They burn cleaner, are more reliable, and get better gas mileage. Now you can ride without leaving a trail of blue smoke.

Baloncici/Dreamstime.com

HOW IT WORKS

An internal combustion engine needs three things to function: fuel, spark, and compression. Each of these components must be present both in the proper amount and at the correct time.

The "fuel" component is actually a mixture of air and fuel, since anything that burns needs air to do so. What might seem surprising is the amount of air required. The ratio of air to fuel by volume in a normally functioning, naturally aspirated four-stroke engine is about 13.2:1. In other words, an engine that runs well uses 13 times more air than fuel.

The "spark" component is just that: an electrical spark. It ignites the air/fuel mixture. The air/fuel mixture is not supposed to explode, but should instead burn in a quick, even manner, causing a controlled yet extreme increase in pressure. This is called the "firing event." It takes place in the combustion chamber.

The "compression" component is determined by the environment inside the combustion chamber, which must be tightly sealed in order to contain as much of the pressure created by the firing event as possible. The air/fuel mixture can be perfect, the spark strong and perfectly timed, but if the combustion chamber leaks, power that could be propelling your scooter is simply evaporating into thin air. Leaks occur from valves that don't seat properly or from worn piston rings or cylinder walls.

THE PISTON ENGINE

In basic terms, a piston engine works like this: A mixture of air and fuel is delivered to a combustion chamber where it is set on fire by an electrical spark, creating a rapid increase in pressure. This pressure acts on a piston, forcing it to move down inside a cylinder. The piston is attached to a crankshaft by a connecting rod. As the piston moves down, it turns the crankshaft. This rotation is transferred to the rear wheel through the torque converter, gearbox, and final drive.

In slightly more complex terms, a piston engine is made up of many components.

The crankshaft is housed in the engine's bottom end. It rides on main bearings, which are bathed in motor oil delivered through passages called "journals." At one end of the crankshaft is the flywheel. This is a big, heavy disc that stores kinetic energy and uses inertia to keep the crankshaft turning. Mounted on the bottom end is the cylinder block, which houses the piston. On top of the cylinder block is the cylinder head. Inside the cylinder head are the intake and exhaust valves. These valves are operated directly by overhead camshafts and rocker arms.

The air/fuel mixture is created in the carburetor and then delivered to the cylinder by way of the intake manifold, intake ports, and intake valves. It is compressed in the combustion chamber by the piston and then ignited by the spark plug. After the mixture has been burned, the residue gases leave the combustion chamber through exhaust valves, exhaust ports, and the exhaust manifold, pipes, mufflers, and catalytic converters.

The combustion chamber is defined at the bottom by the top of the piston, on the side by the cylinder wall, and at the top by the cylinder head.

THE FOUR-STROKE PRINCIPLE

As noted earlier, the fundamental action of an engine is to turn its crankshaft by forcing one or more pistons to move down inside a cylinder. Of course, once a piston has moved down, it must move back up in order to repeat the forcing-down process. As the piston moves fully from the top of the cylinder to the bottom, the crankshaft turns 180 degrees. Turn it 180 degrees more, and the piston is back at the top of the cylinder.

When the piston is as high in the cylinder as it can get, it is at top dead center (TDC). When the piston is as low in the cylinder as it can get, it is at bottom dead center (BDC). The movement of the piston from one end of the cylinder to the other is called a "stroke."

A four-stroke engine operates in a sequence of four consecutive piston strokes that occur during two complete rotations of the crankshaft. Within each stroke, a prescribed sequence of events takes place, and each stroke has its own unique sequence.

Stroke 1: The Intake Stroke

During the intake stroke, the piston moves from TDC down to BDC. As it goes down, the volume in the cylinder above the piston grows. Simultaneously, the intake valves open. A vacuum created by the growing cylinder volume combines with normal atmospheric pressure to push the air/fuel mixture past the open intake valves and into the cylinder.

Stroke 2: The Compression Stroke

During the compression stroke, the piston moves from BDC back up to TDC. As it goes up, it compresses the air/fuel mixture into the combustion chamber. This destabilizes the mixture, preparing it for ignition.

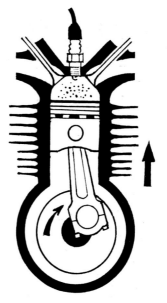

2 Compression
Piston moves from
BDC to TDC.
Both valves are closed.
Piston compresses
mixture.

Stroke 3: The Power Stroke

During the power stroke, the piston moves from TDC back down to BDC. The air/fuel mixture is ignited and the resulting pressure from the burn pushes the piston down. This is the only time the crankshaft is made to turn by energy other than the inertia of the flywheel.

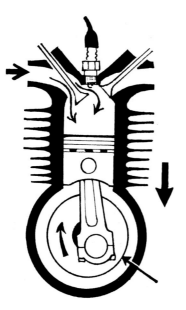

1 Induction
Piston moves from
TDC to BDC.
Intake valves open.
Air/fuel mixture enters
combustion chamber.

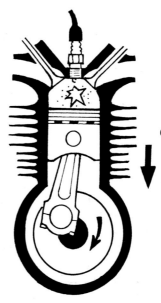

3 Combustion
Piston moves from
TDC to BDC.
The big bang!
Spark plug ignites
compressed mixture.

Stroke 4: The Exhaust Stroke

During the exhaust stroke, the piston moves from BDC back up to TDC. The exhaust valves open, and the waste gases from the firing event are pushed out through the exhaust port and are expelled through the exhaust pipe, muffler, and catalytic converter.

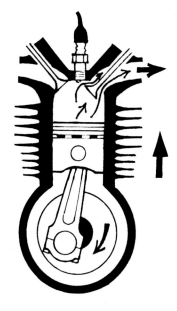

4 Exhaust
Piston moves from BDC to TDC. Exhaust valve opens and burned gases leave chamber.

THE CYLINDER HEAD

Here is where most four-stroke maintenance projects are performed. Scooter engines are pretty tough, so it's likely the only thing you'll ever need to do to the cylinder head is adjust the valves.

As described earlier, the bottom of the cylinder head is the roof of the combustion chamber. It can be in the shape of a dome, or it can have a combination of slants and curves. Embedded in whatever shape the roof takes are the intake and exhaust valve heads. When closed, the valve heads rest against precisely milled areas in the roof of the combustion chamber. These are called the valve seats.

Most modern four-stroke scooter engines use single overhead camshafts. A chain or belt drives the camshaft from the crankshaft, turning the camshaft one half of one rotation for every full rotation of the crankshaft.

Located along the camshaft are the cam lobes, which are, essentially, egg-shaped protuberances. As the camshaft turns,

these protuberances begin to push on rocker arms, which in turn push on the ends of the valves (the valve stems), forcing them down. When the valve stem is pushed down, the valve head is pushed away from the valve seat in the top of the combustion chamber, creating an opening through which the air/fuel mix can enter the cylinder (intake valves), or spent gases can exit (exhaust valves). As the cam lobe releases the valve stem, springs force the valve back into the closed position, resealing the combustion chamber.

When a valve is in the closed position, there is a space between the end of the valve stem and the rocker arm. It is this gap that must be adjusted. Too big a gap, and the rocker arm slams into the valve stem, eventually changing its shape. Too little, and the valve will open too far. If this happens with an exhaust valve, it will run too hot, burning the valve and keeping it from seating properly. This will greatly reduce one of the three things an engine needs in order to run properly: compression.

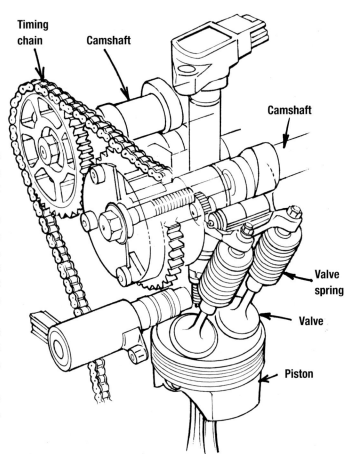

Timing chain
Camshaft
Camshaft
Valve spring
Valve
Piston

PROJECT 5
Valve Adjustment

 Time: 2 hours

 Tools: Wrenches; torque wrench and socket; pliers; flat-blade screwdriver; dead-blow hammer or rubber mallet; flashlight; feeler gauge

 Talent: 4

 Cost: $

 Parts: Valve-cover gasket

 Benefit: Longer tappet and valve-stem lives; quieter engine

1 Remove the seat, under-seat storage bin, and any body panels necessary order to gain access to the engine. (See chapter 13.)

2 Once the engine is accessible, remove the spark-plug wire. Using the proper spark-plug wrench, remove the spark plug.

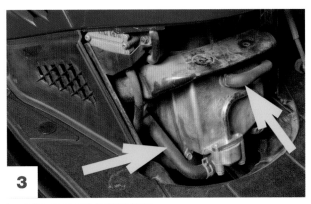

3 Locate the vacuum and air-bypass hoses.

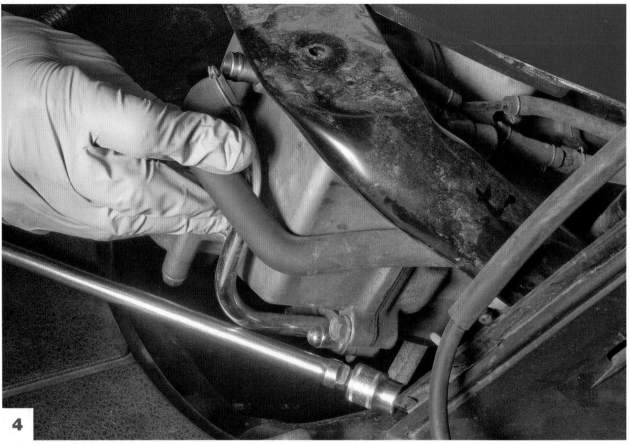

4

Remove the hoses. Use a pair of pliers to release the hose clamp, then work the hose away from the fitting with your hand. Don't use the pliers for this last step or you'll damage the hose.

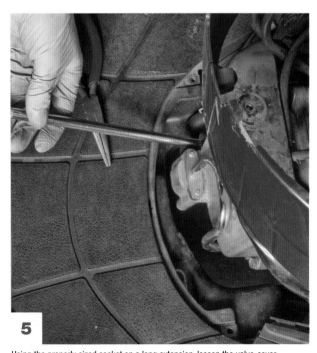

5

Using the properly sized socket on a long extension, loosen the valve-cover retaining bolts.

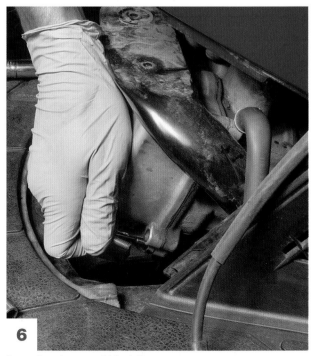

6

Remove the valve-cover retaining bolts.

7 Pry the valve cover away from the cylinder head.

8 Carefully remove the valve cover.

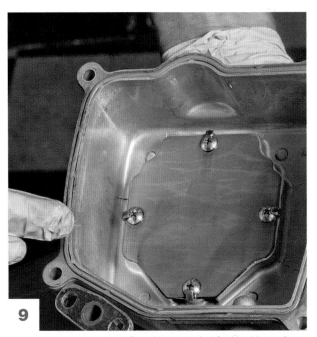

9 Inspect the valve-cover gasket. If it's a rubber gasket, look for rips, nicks, or other signs of wear that might cause leaks. Run your finger along the gasket and feel for imperfections. If it's a paper gasket, don't try to reuse it, just replace it.

10

Clean and inspect valve cover itself. Make sure there are no nicks or other irregularities on the mating surface where the valve cover meets the cylinder head. Clean and inspect the mating surface on the cylinder head.

11

When the piston is at top dead center (TDC) of its compression stroke, the intake and exhaust valves are closed and their rocker arms are at rest. This is the position everything must be in when the valve clearances are adjusted. In order to locate the piston at TDC of the compression stroke, you need to expose the rotor bolt so you can turn the crankshaft. First, remove the cover on the side of the crankcase.

12

When the cover has been removed, you'll see the rotor bolt inside the crankcase.

13

Remove the timing mark cover so you can see the timing marks on the flywheel.

14 Put a properly sized socket on an extension and fix it to the rotor bolt.

15 Rotate the crankshaft in the direction it would turn if the engine were running. Turn it until the TDC mark appears on the flywheel.

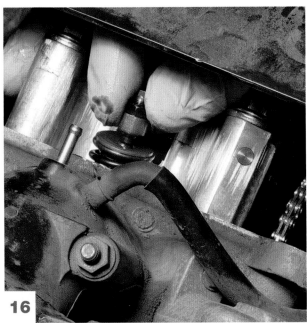

16 Look up the specified valve clearance values in your scooter owner's or service manual. Exhaust valve clearances are typically larger than those of intake valves. Take note of whether the clearances are given as metric or standard values. Locate the valve you want to adjust. Exhaust valves are on the side where the exhaust pipe mounts to the cylinder. Intake valves are on the side where the intake manifold is mounted. Before checking the clearance, lift the rocker arm to make sure it is at the top of its stroke.

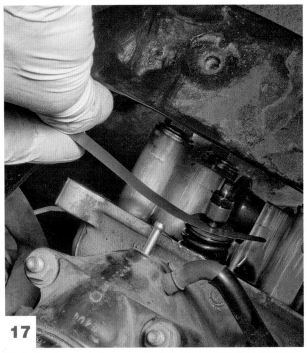

17 Check valve clearances with an appropriately sized feeler gauge. This is the tricky part. Be sure the feeler gauge isn't pushing the valve stem down when it slides through the gap. At the same time, make sure both sides of the feeler gauge make contact—there should be no gaps. You should feel a slight resistance as you slide the feeler gauge back and forth, but it shouldn't be too tight.

18

Adjust the clearance as necessary. First, loosen the tappet locknut with a properly sized wrench.

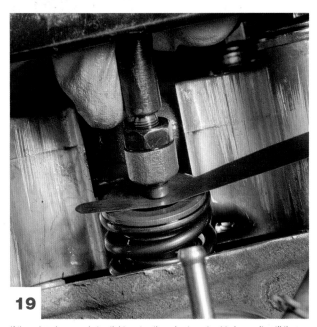

19

If the valve clearance is too tight, screw the valve tappet out to loosen it until the feeler gauge can be inserted. If the clearance is too loose, insert the feeler gauge. Keep the feeler gauge in place as you tighten the tappet. While tightening, slide the gauge back and forth. Tighten until you begin to feel friction on the feeler gauge. Stop when the friction feels right—not too much, but enough to know that you're sliding the gauge between something. Err on the loose side; tight valves run hot and can burn. Too loose and the valvetrain will be damaged, though, so get the clearance as close as you can.

20

While holding the tappet in place with a screwdriver, use a wrench to tighten the locknut to the torque value specified in your scooter's manual. Check your work. It's possible that tightening the locknut loosened the clearance, so be sure it's still right. When all the valve clearances have been adjusted and checked, reassemble everything in the reverse order of disassembly.

PROJECT 6
Engine Compression Test

 Time: 1 hour

 Tools: 4-stroke engine compression gauge

⭐ **Talent:** 2

 Cost: None (yet)

 Parts: None (yet)

 Benefit: Knowledge of how efficiently your engine is running

1 Remove the spark plug (see Project 1, page 14). Insert the compression tester into the spark-plug hole in the cylinder head.

2 Crank the engine 8 to 10 times or until tester reads no higher. Record results and check against the compression value specified in the owner's manual.

3 Remove the tester. Replace the plug (see Project 1, page 14).

Chapter 3
Two-Stroke Engine

Two-stroke engines make power every time the piston goes down. You'd think a two-stroke engine would be twice as powerful as a four-stroke engine of the same displacement, since four-strokes only make power every other time the piston goes down, but that's not the case. Almost, but not quite. They're still pretty fast, as you can see by the fancy paint job.

HOW IT WORKS

Two-stroke and four-stroke scooter engines are similar in many ways. They both have crankcases, cylinders, cylinder heads, pistons, and crankshafts. They both have carburetors and exhaust systems. They both burn gasoline in order to push a piston down and turn a crankshaft, which ultimately turns your scooter's rear wheel. But they function in fundamentally different ways. In fact, they're so different that many competent four-stroke mechanics refer to two-stroke tuning as a black art.

This difference is in the gasoline-burning event. Both types of engine use a spark plug to ignite an air/fuel mixture, but one ignites its air/fuel mixture twice as often as the other. Four-stroke engines burn fuel every other full revolution of the crankshaft. Two-stroke engines burn fuel every time the crankshaft turns one full revolution.

When a piston is at the very top of its travel through the cylinder, it is known as being at top dead center (TDC). When a piston is at the very bottom of its travel through the cylinder, it is at bottom dead center (BDC). A stroke is

defined as when the piston goes from TDC to BDC, or from BDC to TDC. Each stroke requires one-half of one rotation of the crankshaft.

To realize the same number of events (intake, compression, combustion, and exhaust) in half the number of strokes, more than one event must take place during each stroke. Thus, when the piston goes from TDC to BDC, combustion, exhaust, and intake events take place. As the piston goes from BDC back to TDC, exhaust, intake, and compression events occur. This bundling of events during the down and up strokes requires precise design and manufacture of all two-stroke engine components. It also means that a certain amount of unburned air/fuel mixture is going to go directly out the exhaust pipe.

STRENGTHS AND WEAKNESSES

Every time a two-stroke engine's piston descends, it is being pushed down by the compression event. By contrast, a four-stroke engine's piston is pushed down by the combustion event only every other time it descends. Therefore, two-stroke engines create more power than four-stroke engines of the same size. Not quite twice as much, as one might think, but pretty close. However, this extra power comes at an emissions price. Two-stroke engines pump out a lot more exhaust gasses than four-stroke engines do. So much more, in fact, that they can't meet many government pollution control agency engine emission requirements. Therefore, two-stroke engines have been rather rapidly phased out of production since the turn of the century. A few new scooters are still available with small (50cc) two-stroke engines, but not many.

Since two-stroke and four-stroke engines function in fundamentally different ways, they must be designed with basic differences. These differences involve air/fuel intake and exhaust methods.

While four-stroke engines use poppet valves located in the cylinder head to regulate intake and exhaust, two-stroke engines do not. The intake and exhaust ports are basically just holes in the cylinder walls. There might be some sort of valve regulating what gets through the intake port hole, but two-stroke engines rely on exhaust-pipe design to suck exhaust gasses out the exhaust port hole. The poppet valves of four-stroke engine intake-and-exhaust systems are far more precise.

Another difference is that while four-stroke engine bottom ends (crankshaft and main bearings, connecting rods and rod bearings) operate in a bath of oil augmented by journals that squirt more oil onto moving parts, two-stroke engine bottom ends rely entirely on the air/fuel mixture to provide lubrication. So the air/fuel mixture also contains oil. This contributes further to the intensity of exhaust emissions that come out of two-stroke engines. Not only is there unburned air/fuel mixture in the exhaust, there's a certain amount of burned oil.

The fact that oil must be added to the air/fuel mixture and is eventually burned in the combustion chamber means that the combustion chamber and spark plug get covered in soot. This soot must be cleaned periodically, which involves removing not only the spark plug but the whole cylinder head. Fortunately, two-stroke cylinder heads are pretty much just a slab of aluminum held in place by some bolts, so they're pretty easy to remove. If you can get access to them.

Two-stroke engines also consume more fuel than four-stroke engines of the same size. First, every down stroke of the piston is a power stroke. Second, a portion of the exhaust gas is made up of unburned fuel.

If there was a way to more precisely meter two-stroke intake and exhaust, one could have the power of a two-stroke engine without its typical billowing cloud of emissions. Actually, there is a way to more precisely meter the intake part of the equation. It's called direct injection and has led to a slight resurgence of two-stroke motorcycle engines. The system is rather complex, however, and hasn't yet made its way to scooters.

CRANKCASE AND CYLINDER

As discussed earlier, a two-stroke engine's air/fuel mixture is augmented with two-stroke oil in order to lubricate the bottom end. This leads to one of the peculiarities of the two-stroke engine: The carburetor is mounted on an intake port that goes into the crankcase. The air/fuel mixture is still drawn through the carburetor by a combination of atmospheric pressure and vacuum created by the piston going down in its cylinder, but the mixture goes through the crankcase on its way to the combustion chamber.

Beyond the intake port into the crankcase, there are more ports leading from the crankcase to the cylinder. These ports open into the cylinder wall at the bottom of the combustion chamber, just above the top of the piston when it's at BDC. The exhaust port is across from the intake port on the other side of the cylinder wall, at a slightly higher level. All of these ports must be carefully designed to prevent the incoming air/fuel mixture from simply going straight from the intake port into the exhaust port. The process by which the mixture is drawn into most two-stroke scooter combustion chambers is an effect called loop scavenging.

Although some of the mixture will inevitably go directly out the exhaust port, the geometry of a properly designed loop-scavenging two-stroke engine ensures that most of the incoming air and fuel swirls upward, becoming trapped in the combustion chamber after the piston has risen in the cylinder far enough to block the intake and exhaust ports. The mixture bounces off the combustion chamber roof as it is compressed by the roof of the upward-moving piston, the spark plug ignites the mixture, it burns and expands, and the piston is forced back down. As the piston goes back down, it begins to expose the exhaust port opening, and the spent gasses are drawn out of the combustion chamber by the geometry of a well-designed exhaust pipe. As the piston continues its descent in the cylinder, the intake port opening begins to be exposed, air/fuel mixture is drawn into the cylinder, and the process repeats itself.

Geometry is of paramount importance in two-stroke engine design. Altering the geometry of the ports and combustion chamber roof can yield performance gains, but most likely will just lead to a poorer-running scooter. Bolting on an exhaust pipe with better geometry is a better bet for improving performance, but remember that improved exhaust flow requires improved intake volume, which can lead right back to the perils of altering port geometry.

INLET VALVES

Originally, a two-stroke engine's air/fuel mixture's flow from the carburetor to the combustion chamber was only impeded when the piston blocked the intake port. However, this was an extremely inefficient method for an inherently inefficient design. Because the interior of a crankcase is always going to have less pressure than whatever ambient air pressure exists outside the crankcase walls, the crankcase itself will always draw an air/fuel mixture from the carburetor. Even when the piston is blocking the intake port, impeding mixture flow to the combustion chamber, fuel is being consumed. In a way, this is a good thing. The bottom end gets its lubrication from the air/fuel mixture, so more of it coming into the crankcase means more lubrication. But it's also wasted gas.

Inlet valves were invented to interrupt the air/fuel mixture flow. Reed valves do this between the carburetor and the crankcase; rotary valves do this on the inside of the crankcase.

Reed valves are exactly what they sound like: a reed or series of reeds that are sucked open when crankcase vacuum is augmented by combustion chamber vacuum as the piston opens the intake port. This allows the air/fuel mixture to be drawn into the intake system in bursts, rather than continuously.

Rotary valves are attached to the crankshaft and open and close the intake port according to where in its rotation the crankshaft happens to be. This achieves the same delivery-in-bursts effect, but in a more precise manner than the reed valve.

However, reed valves are accessible by taking off the carburetor and intake manifold. To get to a rotary valve, you have to get into the bottom end of the engine—a job that requires "splitting the engine," which simply means taking off the crankcase side covers. Unfortunately, "simply" and "taking off the crankcase side covers" should never appear together in the same sentence.

OIL PUMP

In a two-stroke, motor oil to lubricate the engine's bottom end is part of the air/fuel mixture. The oil is introduced to the mixture by adding it to the gas in the gas tank, or by injecting it into the air/fuel mixture after it leaves the carburetor. The first method requires that you carry around a bottle of two-stroke oil and pour it into the tank when you refuel. Alternately, you could mix the gas and oil in a gas can. This allows you to make sure the gas and oil are properly mixed, but it also requires that you either carry around the gas can or only refuel at home.

Because adding two-stroke oil to the gas before it gets to the carburetor is cumbersome, not to mention the added residue left in carb jets and passages, your two-stroke scooter probably uses the injection method of adding oil to the air/fuel mixture. This requires an oil pump.

Oil pumps are operated either by a cable or a belt. In a cable-operated system, a cable is attached to the throttle cable, so pump speed increases as the throttle is opened. Since all cables eventually stretch, the oil pump cable must be adjusted periodically. Check your owner's manual for the procedure for your scooter. Belt-driven oil pumps are driven by a belt that connects the pump to the crankshaft via a pulley. The faster the crankshaft turns, the faster the pump turns. This is a good system, but belts can break. If this happens while you're riding, you'll soon experience catastrophic engine failure if you don't stop. Check the oil-pump belt condition periodically, and replace it at the intervals recommended in your owner's manual.

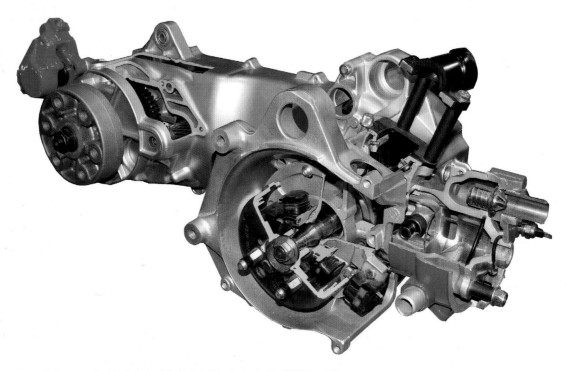

In times past, two-strokes were prized for their simplicity. Today nothing is simple. *Zmaj011/Dreamstime.com*

PROJECT 7
Top End Rebuild

 Time: 3 hours

 Tools: Wrenches; torque wrench and socket; pliers; dead-blow hammer or rubber mallet; a supply of rags or paper towels; gasket scraper or single-sided razor blade; wire brush; nylon scrubbing pad

 Talent: 4

 Cost: $$

 Parts: Valve-cover gasket; cylinder base gasket; cleaning solvent; piston rings; two-stroke oil

 Benefit: An engine that runs like new

This project is actually comprised of four separate procedures: Removing and reinstalling the cylinder head; decarbonizing the cylinder head; removing, cleaning, and reinstalling the cylinder; and replacing the piston rings. On most two-stroke scooters, the cylinder head and the cylinder itself are held in place by the same mounting bolts. This means that, when you remove the cylinder head, the cylinder also comes loose from the crankcase, relieving pressure on the cylinder-base gasket. So the base gasket must then be replaced, even if you were just planning to remove only the cylinder head. In order to replace the base gasket, the old gasket must be scraped off the cylinder and crankcase mating surfaces. You have to remove the cylinder in order to do that. While the cylinder is removed and the piston is exposed, you might as well take the opportunity to clean the piston dome and change the rings.

In order to show this project more clearly, the engine has been removed from the scooter. You don't have to do this, but it does make the job a lot easier.

As you can see, when you remove the engine, you might also be removing a good deal more. This is because, in typical modern scooter design, the left side of the crankcase is cast as a part that also includes the inner half of the drive-belt housing. And cast into the other end of the inner half of the drive-belt housing is the drivebox. So, when you remove the engine, you are also, by necessity of design, removing the inner half of the drive-belt housing and the drivebox. To make matters still more interesting, the lower mount of the rear shock absorber attaches to a tab molded into the upper portion of the back half of the inner drive-belt cover. In essence, the whole unit—engine, inner drive-belt cover, and drivebox—serves as the rear swingarm. Which, incidentally, means two things: The engine changes position every time you go over a bump, and the drive-belt cover is a stressed member of the suspension. Therefore, tightening the drive-belt cover mounting bolts to the proper torque value is a must.

1 Start by removing the exhaust system (see Project 11). Next, disconnect any hoses and wires that are attached to the cylinder head. Begin with the spark-plug wire, then remove the spark plug.

2 Loosen the cylinder-head/cylinder mounting bolts. Do this evenly and in a criss-cross pattern. Start with one bolt and loosen it a quarter of a turn. Then go diagonally across the cylinder head and loosen that bolt the same amount. Repeat this procedure with the last two bolts.

3

After all the bolts have been loosened, remove them completely.

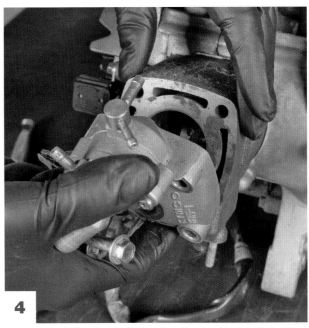

4

Remove the head. Since the bolts that hold the cylinder head in place also hold the cylinder in place, the cylinder will be loose now too. The base gasket will probably hold it in place, but even if it comes loose, the piston inside the cylinder bore should keep the cylinder from just falling off. Even so, be careful the cylinder does not fall off after the mounting bolts are removed. Set the cylinder head aside for cleaning and inspection later.

5

Remove the cylinder. You might need to knock it loose from the crankcase with a soft rubber mallet or a dead-blow hammer.

6

Carefully slide the cylinder away from the crankcase, and off of the piston inside the cylinder bore. Don't let the piston fall against anything as it comes out of the cylinder bore. Set the cylinder aside for cleaning and inspection later.

7

Stuff clean rags in the hole in the crankcase to prevent bits of gasket, cleaning solvent, or anything else from getting inside the crankcase.

8

Clean the cylinder head. Start by scraping off the old gasket or any remnants of it. A gasket scraper will work, but a single-sided razor blade does the job better and with less chance of wrecking the head. The head is made of aluminum, and aluminum is very soft and easily damaged.

9

Next, spray cleaning solvent all over the head—top, bottom, and sides. Brake cleaner or contact cleaner works best for this.

10

Scrub the surfaces with a wire brush. Brass bristles are best, but stainless bristles will work. Again, be careful not to gouge the aluminum. Brush lightly but firmly.

47

11

Rinse the head with cleaner.

12

Dry off the head with a rag or a paper towel. Any excess cleaner left on the head will just become newly burned residue the next time the engine is started, defeating the purpose of the cleaning you just did.

13

Inspect the head. Look for cracks, nicks, gouges, or other irregularities, especially on the roof of the combustion chamber and on the mating surface where the cylinder head meets the cylinder. Make sure there are no chunks of the old gasket still stuck to the mating surface. Spray more cleaner on the bottom of the head and dress the surface with an abrasive nylon scrubbing pad.

14

Rinse the head with cleaner again, and wipe it dry. Inspect the head again. When you are convinced it is clean, dry, and free of imperfections, set it aside.

15

Check the piston wrist-pin bearing for play. Grab the piston and try to move it. A little side-to-side play is okay, but up-and-down play is not.

16

Clean the piston. First, remove the piston rings. A piston ring doesn't form an enclosed circle, but rather is shaped like an extreme "C." Locate the ends of the top ring.

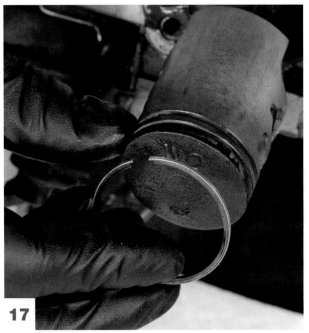

17

Gently spread the ends apart until the ring can be removed from the groove in the piston. Be careful not to bend or twist the ring if you plan to reuse it. Remove the bottom ring in the same manner. Consult your scooter's service manual for the proper ring end-gap specifications before removing each ring. Do not reuse rings that are beyond tolerances. Rings are cheap; you're best off just replacing them as a matter of course.

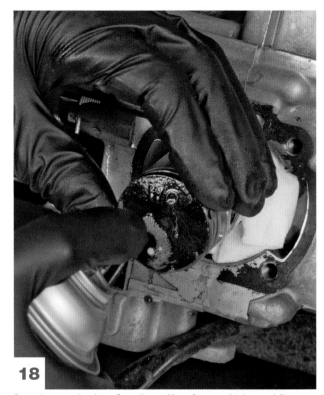

18

Spray cleaner on the piston. Cover the outside surface completely, especially the dome.

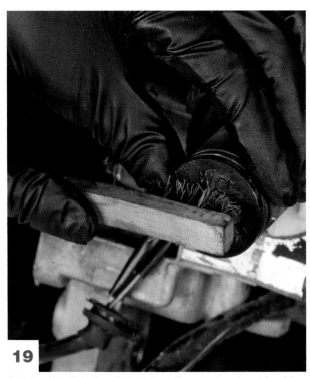

19

Scrub the piston, first with a wire brush, then with an abrasive nylon scrub pad. Do this carefully. Be sure to get in the ring grooves. Repeat this process a few times until the dome of the piston is as clean as it can get. Wipe off any excess cleaner and inspect the piston for imperfections, especially cracks and scoring.

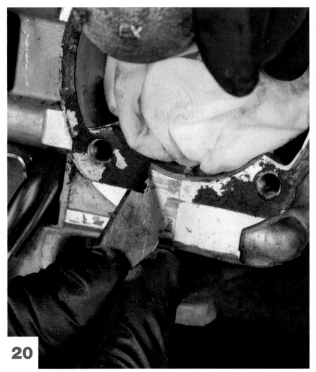

20

Carefully clean the crankcase mating surface where it meets the cylinder base. Scrape off the old gasket (or any remnants of it) with a razor blade, then clean the mating surface by spraying it with solvent and scrubbing it with a wire brush and an abrasive nylon scrub pad. Wipe off any excess cleaner.

21

Clean the cylinder. Scrape any gasket remnants from the top and bottom mating surfaces, then clean the mating surfaces by spraying them with solvent and scrubbing them with a wire brush and an abrasive nylon scrub pad.

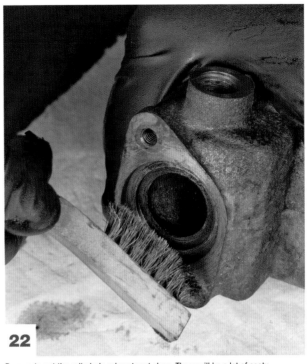

22

Be sure to get the cylinder's exhaust port clean. There will be a lot of sooty residue on the outside, where the exhaust pipe mounts. If this area is not cleaned thoroughly, the exhaust pipe will not seat properly against the cylinder, the exhaust gasket will not seat properly when the exhaust pipe is reattached, or both.

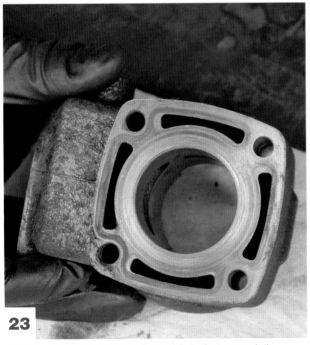

23

Inspect the cylinder for imperfections. Pay special attention to gouges in the top and bottom mating surfaces, scoring on the cylinder bore wall, and carbon buildup around the exhaust port. This would be a good time to take the cylinder to a shop and have them check the bore diameter to see if it is still within allowable tolerances. If it isn't, it can be rebored or replaced. When reboring or replacing the cylinder, always replace the piston at the same time.

24

Install the new rings or, if you have to, the old rings. First, locate the separating pin in each of the piston's ring grooves. The separating pin will go between the ends of the ring when it is installed.

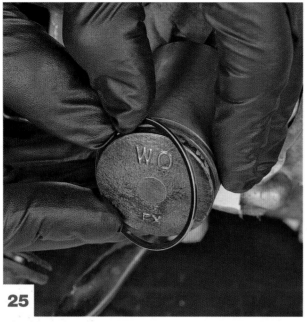

25

Pay attention to which ring goes in what groove. Consult your scooter's service manual. Sometimes one or both of the rings are chrome, sometimes neither is. Typically, if one of the rings is chrome, it goes in the top groove. Carefully spread the bottom ring and slide it over the piston and into the bottom groove. Don't spread it too much or twist it. Make sure the locating pin is between the ends of the ring. Repeat this procedure for the top ring.

26

Reinstall the cylinder. First, remove the rag from the hole in the crankcase, then coat the piston skirts with two-stroke oil.

27

Coat the cylinder walls with two-stroke oil.

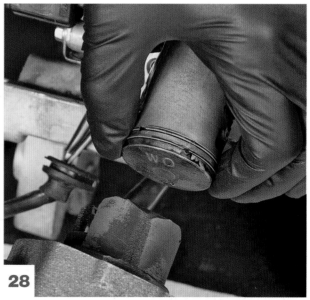

28

Install a new cylinder base gasket onto the bottom of the cylinder, then slide the cylinder over the piston. Notice that the rings stick out from the piston skirt. This is because they do their job by exerting pressure on the cylinder wall. Therefore, in order to slide the cylinder over the piston, you must compress the rings into their grooves completely. Ring-compressing tools are available, but this is a tiny single-cylinder engine, so you should be able to do compress the rings with your fingers. Be sure the locating pin stays between the ring ends. This is a potentially aggravating job, since the rings keep trying to pop back out. But, with a bit of patience and a plan, it can be done. Start with the top ring. When it is completely inside the cylinder, compress the bottom ring and work that one into the cylinder.

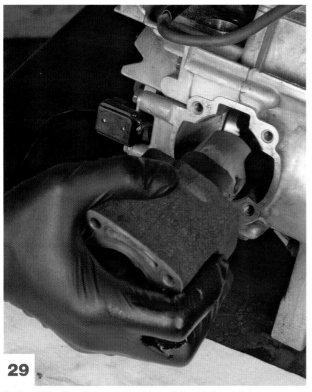

29

Continue sliding the cylinder over the piston until it meets the crankcase.

30

Install a new cylinder head gasket onto the cylinder head and reinstall the cylinder head onto the cylinder.

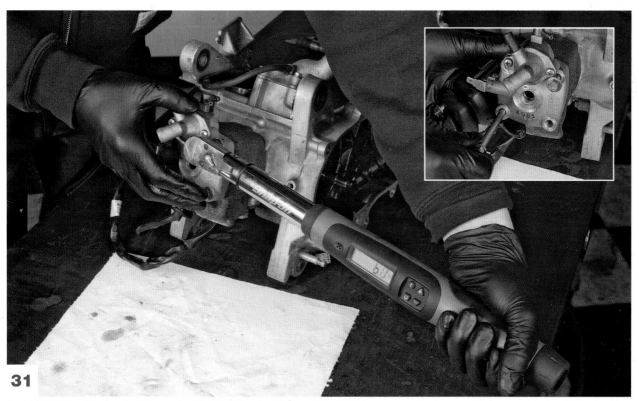

31

Inset: Reinstall the cylinder-head/cylinder mounting bolts. Screw them in until they are finger tight, then use a wrench. Do not overtighten them at this stage. Tighten the bolts evenly, a little at a time and in a crisscross pattern. *Main picture:* Torque the cylinder-head/cylinder mounting bolts to the torque value specified in your scooter owner's or service manual. Do this in a crisscross pattern.

Chapter 4
Engine Cooling System

Liquid-cooled scooter engines last longer. It's that simple.

HOW IT WORKS

Scooter engines burn gasoline to produce horsepower, and gasoline burns at high temperatures, generally between 880 and 1,040 degrees Fahrenheit. The auto-ignite temperature of gas is 536 degrees Fahrenheit. Therefore, in order to control the combustion process by igniting the air/fuel mixture with the spark plug, scooter engines need a process through which they cool themselves.

Heat generated by the combustion process must be carried away from the combustion chamber somehow. Dissipation is the root of all scooter engine-cooling systems. First, heat spreads from the atmosphere inside the cylinder to the cylinder walls. From there, it flows into the rest of the engine components, but it is the heat absorbed by the cylinder walls that concerns us. This heat must be dissipated. There are two ways to dissipate heat from the cylinder walls: through air and through liquid.

In the first type of system, air-cooling, heat is absorbed by the cylinder walls. It then radiates outward through fins

cast into the outside of the cylinder walls. These fins allow the outside surface of the cylinder wall to contact much more air and therefore dissipate much more heat. Of course, for this process to remain effective, the air into which the heat is dissipated must be continually replaced. If the cylinder is exposed to air rushing by as the scooter moves down the road, replacement is not an issue. Most scooter engines are enclosed, however, and must rely on a fan to replenish the supply of fresh cool air.

Liquid-cooled engines work in basically the same way as do air-cooled engines, except that the heat absorbed by the cylinder walls is transferred to liquid instead of air. Actually, air is used to dissipate heat in liquid-cooled systems too. As the liquid coolant flows through the radiator, heat is transferred from the liquid into cooling fins and then dissipates into the air surrounding the fins—but we're getting ahead of ourselves.

Cylinders of liquid-cooled engines contain water jackets, through which the liquid coolant circulates. Heat absorbed by the cylinder wall dissipates into the liquid coolant. As with the air surrounding an air-cooled engine's cooling fins, the liquid coolant in the cylinder's water jacket must be continually replaced in order to remain effective. So liquid-cooling systems employ a pump to move the liquid coolant from the water jacket to the radiator and back to the water jacket.

STRENGTHS AND WEAKNESSES

Air cooling is simple. All that's needed are cooling fins on the outside of the cylinder wall and a continually replenished supply of air, either by exposure or a fan. The downside is that air cooling is much harder to control. Air-cooled engines run hotter on hot days, and there's not much anyone can do about it. And, when traffic gets thick, scooter speeds slow and less air rushes by. Air-cooled engines must be designed to accommodate inevitable fluctuations in operating temperature. This basically comes down to larger manufacturing tolerances. In other words, there's more slop between parts.

Since there's no real way to control the temperature range in which an air-cooled engine will operate—some will go to the Arctic; others will go to the equator—engineers focus on what they *can* control when designing an engine. For example, pistons expand as they get hot. Not knowing exactly how hot a piston might get, an engineer will specify a manufacturing tolerance large enough to allow the piston to expand to whatever size it might get powering a scooter in Kenya, yet still small enough to create compression when powering a scooter in Alaska.

Liquid cooling is far more controllable, but much more complex. When working properly, a liquid-cooling system can maintain engine-operating temperatures that stay within defined boundaries, allowing engineers to design engine parts within much tighter tolerances. As is always the case, however, the more pieces a system employs, the more things there are to go wrong.

The system must be airtight. Leaks deplete liquid coolant supplies, contaminate and corrode other parts, and generally weaken the pressurized system. Plus, they leave unsightly stains on the garage floor. So hoses and gaskets must retain their integrity, and passages within the engine itself can't have cracks. The system's pump must operate properly. Freshly cooled coolant must always be making its way from the radiator to the cylinder's water jacket, and coolant that has absorbed heat from the cylinder walls must always be going to the radiator to dissipate that heat. The thermostat has to be able to maintain proper engine operating temperatures. And, of course, the liquid coolant itself must be fresh enough to do its job. Old coolant loses its ability to absorb heat; really old coolant can even develop an electrostatic charge, leading to severe corrosion within aluminum engine components. Liquid coolant without enough anti-freeze can freeze in the winter, cracking cylinders and rupturing hoses and radiators.

AIR-COOLING SYSTEMS

Air-cooling systems are quite simple. The only parts that can fail are the fan motor, the fan blades, the fan temperature sensor, and the fan motor switch—all assuming the system even employs a fan. Of course, the air ducts must remain open, but that's simply a matter of keeping them free of debris. This is the first area to check if your air-cooled scooter's engine overheats.

If the ducts are able to furnish a steady supply of fresh air, the next thing to check is the fan. Does the fan turn on? If it does, check the condition of the fan blades. If they are broken or cracked, replace them. If the fan does not turn on when it is supposed to, check the fan temperature sensor. If the fan does not turn on at all, check the fan motor relay switch. If the relay switch works properly, check the fan motor itself. Replace whatever parts aren't working.

LIQUID-COOLING SYSTEMS

Liquid-cooling systems are quite a bit more complex and incorporate a number of parts. Hoses, junctions, gaskets, passageways, thermostats, pumps, radiators, radiator caps, reservoirs, temperature sensors, and the coolant liquid itself must all function as they are supposed to. The first thing to do when troubleshooting liquid-cooling systems is to flush and refill the system with new coolant.

Visually inspect the system. Are there any leaks from cracked or improperly sealed hoses? Even cracked hoses that aren't leaking should be replaced, since they'll eventually fail. Is coolant seeping past joints between engine components? Simply retorqueing bolts that hold the components together could solve the problem. If that doesn't work, the gasket itself will have to be replaced. Check the oil. Does it appear foamy or discolored? This could indicate an improperly sealed head gasket or, worse, a cracked cylinder.

Check the radiator itself. Make certain that nothing is blocking the air passage to the radiator—especially aftermarket accessories or bodywork. Make certain that the radiator is not plugged with bugs, mud, or other debris.

Check the pump. If it works, but coolant isn't circulating, there's an obstruction in the system. Clean or replace hoses, and ensure passageways in the engine aren't blocked. If the pump works, make sure it's circulating the amount of coolant it's supposed to. Look in the service manual for pump specifications and then test the pump. A weak pump won't replenish the cylinder's water jacket with a supply of freshly cooled coolant quickly enough. This presents a compound problem: Not only does liquid do a good job of transferring heat, but liquid makes a pretty good insulator. So, as the coolant gets hotter, it loses its ability to absorb heat from the cylinder wall—plus it helps the cylinder wall retain heat. If the pump works according to its prescribed specifications, check the thermostat. If the thermostat isn't opening when it's supposed to, coolant won't circulate. Finally, if there's a fan on the radiator, see if it's working. Follow the steps for checking fans listed in the air-cooled systems section of this chapter.

PROJECT 8
Check Engine Cooling System—
Liquid Cooling

 Time: 2 hours

 Tools: Wrenches; funnel; a supply of rags or paper towels

 Talent: 2

 Cost: $

 Parts: Engine coolant

 Benefit: A properly functioning engine cooling system

1

Liquid-cooling systems for scooter engines are complex affairs. Draining, flushing, filling, and bleeding your scooter engine's liquid-cooling system takes a few hours and some special tools, and you'll wreck your engine if you don't get it right the first time. It's best to leave the job to a professional mechanic; check your owner's manual for service intervals. You can, however, conduct regular visual inspections to make sure everything is in working order. Start by checking the level in the coolant reservoir.

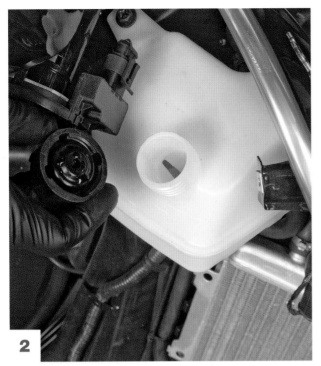

2

You might need to remove a panel to expose the coolant reservoir. (See chapter 13.) The reservoir has two lines molded into it: The upper line shows the maximum level when the coolant is hot; the lower line shows the minimum level when the coolant is cold. Check the level when the coolant is cold. If it is below the minimum level, add more coolant. First, unscrew the reservoir cap and set it aside.

3

Coolant comes in two forms: concentrated and diluted. You should never use coolant in its concentrated form. Mix concentrated coolant only with distilled water; tap water will introduce contaminants into the system. Check your scooter owner's or service manual for the proper ratio of coolant to water for your typical-use conditions. Diluted coolant typically comes with a 50/50 ratio. Carefully pour the properly diluted coolant into the reservoir. Coolant is harmful to plastic, paint, metal, rubber, and just about everything else your scooter is made of, so don't spill any. When the proper amount of coolant is in the reservoir, reinstall the reservoir cap.

4

Liquid-cooling systems are closed systems, so engine coolant shouldn't just disappear. A small amount evaporates during normal use, but if you need to add significant amounts of coolant on a regular basis, there's a leak somewhere in the system. Liquid-cooling systems are also pressurized systems, so leaks mean the system can't possibly be properly pressurized, therefore it can't possibly function the way it's supposed to. There are hoses that lead from the reservoir to the radiator, hoses that lead from the radiator to the engine, and hoses that lead from the engine back to the radiator. If your scooter has two radiators, there are hoses between them too. And most of these hoses have at least one junction in them; some have more. Leaks can be the result of holes in hoses, corroded junctions, malfunctioning hose clamps, or holes in the radiator. To find the leak, you'll need to remove some body panels and expose the whole system—from the reservoir, to the radiator(s), to the engine, and back to the radiator(s). After the system is completely exposed, start the engine and look for leaks. If you find any, don't put the body panels back on. Just take your scooter to the shop for repairs. This will save you from paying the shop to take them back off again. First inspect the radiator(s).

5

Next, inspect the hoses. Start with the hoses that enter and exit the radiator(s).

6

Finally, inspect the hoses where they enter and exit the engine.

Chapter 5
Fuel-Induction System

A carburetor isn't just a means of mixing air and fuel on the way to the combustion chamber. It's also a place to mount a fancy chrome air cleaner.

HOW IT WORKS

An engine needs three things to function properly: a mixture of air and fuel, a spark to ignite the air/fuel mixture, and compression to utilize the burning air/fuel mixture. The first part of the process is creating the mixture of air and fuel and delivering it to the combustion chamber. Of course, it can't be just any mixture of fuel and air. The air/fuel mix must be of a specific ratio, and it must be consistently delivered to the combustion chamber, in varying volumes, at that ratio.

Combustion requires oxygen. When your scooter burns gasoline, carbon molecules from the gasoline join with oxygen molecules in the air after the air/fuel mixture is ignited by the spark plug. The more oxygen there is in an air/fuel mixture,

the farther apart the carbon molecules are spaced. At a certain point, the distance between the carbon molecules becomes so great that the air/fuel mixture simply can't ignite. Conversely, the less oxygen there is in the air/fuel mixture, the lower the number of carbon molecules that can find oxygen molecules with which to combine. In other words, when there isn't enough oxygen, some of the gasoline in the air/fuel mixture goes unburned. Rich fuel mixtures will always burn if there's at least some oxygen—that's why we don't smoke around open gasoline containers—but they leave behind coatings of carbon that cling to valves, combustion-chamber roofs and walls, pistons and rings, and spark plugs.

The perfect air/fuel ratio is one in which all the oxygen molecules combine with all the carbon molecules, leaving an excess of neither after combustion. This is called a stoichiometric ratio. All fuels have a stoichiometric ratio. As examples, the stoichiometric ratio for natural gas is 17.2 parts air to 1 part gas; propane is 15.5:1, diesel is 14.6:1; and ethanol is 9:1. Gasoline's stoichiometric ratio is 14.7:1. Think about it: For every gallon of gasoline your scooter engine consumes, it also consumes 14.7 gallons of air. Air/fuel mixtures with more than 14.7 parts air to 1 part gasoline are called "lean"; mixtures with less than 14.7 parts air to 1 part gasoline are called "rich."

Lean air/fuel mixtures can cause problems ranging from engine misfires to catastrophic piston failures. Rich air/fuel mixtures foul spark plugs, coat everything inside the combustion chamber with, basically, soot, and leave unburned gasoline to be pushed through the exhaust system and out into the atmosphere. Notice that the possible consequences of rich air/fuel mixtures don't include catastrophic failure of any kind. The worst that will happen is things will get dirty; the only parts that will need replacement are spark plugs. Therefore, it's better to err on the rich side of stoichiometric rather than the lean side. In fact, slightly rich will actually yield more power than stoichiometric, but your scooter will burn more gas and you'll change spark plugs more frequently.

So how does your scooter engine get its supply of consistently blended air and fuel? As the piston begins to descend in the cylinder on its intake stroke, atmospheric pressure combines with the vacuum created by the descending piston to push air into the airbox, where it passes through the

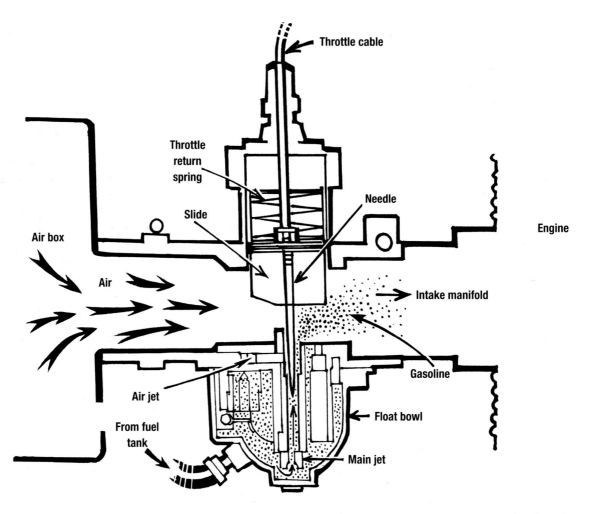

The inner workings of a carburetor.

air filter. The air then goes through the carburetor, into the intake manifold, through the intake port and valves in the cylinder head and into the combustion chamber. It is when the air passes through the carburetor that fuel is added.

A pump feeds fuel through the fuel line from the gas tank to the carburetor, where it is collected in the float bowl. The level of fuel in the float bowl is regulated by a seat valve that is opened and closed by floats that ride on the surface of the fuel in the float bowl. As fuel leaves the float bowl to be combined with air passing through the carburetor on the way to the combustion chamber, the level of fuel in the float bowl decreases, the floats go down, and the seat valve metering the flow of gas into the float bowl opens. As the float bowl fills with gas, the float bowl floats rise until they close the seat valve.

The airbox, which houses the air filter, is attached to the carburetor's throttle body. Directly inside the throttle body is the throttle valve. This is either a butterfly valve or a slide valve. A butterfly valve is a thin, circular sheet of metal that rotates from closed (blocking the throttle passage completely because it is perpendicular to airflow) to open (parallel to airflow); a slide valve simply slides up and down to open or close the throttle passage. Both types of valves are controlled by the throttle cable. As you rotate your scooter's twist grip, the throttle cable opens the throttle valve (or shuts, depending on which direction you're moving the grip), allowing air to rush out of the airbox, through the throttle passage, out of the carburetor, and into the intake manifold.

Airflow through the carburetor is enhanced by a physical principle known as the venturi effect. Essentially, the venturi effect says that a volume of liquid or gas passing from a more restrictive passage to a less restrictive one will speed up, causing a drop in pressure immediately after the transition. At a point somewhere near its middle, the throttle body narrows, then opens up again. This is called the "venturi," because it creates a venturi effect. The point of the exercise is to create vacuum from the aforementioned drop in pressure. It is this vacuum that draws fuel into the airflow, creating the air/fuel mixture that burns in the combustion chamber.

Also embedded in the carburetor body are a number of other passageways. They are much smaller than the throttle passageway, and it is through these passages that fuel is delivered from the float bowl. Since the passages are built into the carburetor body during the casting process, they can only be made to certain tolerances. Not only that, but the atmosphere itself contains different amounts of oxygen at different altitudes. And, of course, your scooter's engine will require different volumes of air/fuel mixture, depending on how hard you're making it work. Since the difference between a 14.7:1 air/fuel mixture and a 15.3:1 mixture can be destructive under heavy loads, fuel delivery must be minutely controllable. This is accomplished by intersecting the fuel-delivery passages with needle valves that screw in or out to restrict or open the passages, or by screwing specifically sized nozzles, called "jets," onto the ends of the passages.

The fuel-delivery passages enter the throttle passage just after the venturi. As the air rushes through the throttle opening, the venturi effect creates vacuum at the ends of the fuel-delivery passages. This vacuum draws fuel into the airflow, where it is vaporized and dispersed into many, many tiny droplets. The tinier the droplets, the more effective the combustion process will be. Since the vaporization process is so important, much care goes into designing carburetors to get droplets that are as small and evenly dispersed as they can possibly be as they're sucked into the air flow.

The newly created air/fuel mixture flows out of the carburetor and into the intake manifold. It's crucial that intake manifolds are designed properly, since abrupt changes in direction will destroy the carefully constructed suspension of fuel droplets in the airflow. The intake manifold delivers the air/fuel mixture to the engine's intake port. The intake port leads to the combustion chamber, where the air/fuel mixture is finally ignited by the spark plug, creating a flame that builds pressure and pushes the piston down on its power stroke.

STRENGTHS AND WEAKNESSES

Carburetors have been around as long as internal combustion engines have required air/fuel mixtures. Pretty much all the bugs have been worked out and, aside from periodic cleaning, properly adjusted carburetors can be left alone. Carburetors are purely mechanical devices that rely on the laws of physics. There is no magic involved. They can be removed, disassembled, cleaned, reassembled, and reinstalled. Adjustments can be made by turning screws and changing jets. Anyone with a set of hand tools can do these things. The only thing you might need a laptop computer for is downloading service manual pages and looking up part numbers. But, for the most part, scooter carburetors can be left adjusted as they were when they left the factories.

On the other hand, a properly adjusted carburetor is, essentially, the best possible set of compromises to be found. Different systems within the carburetor control its functions at different times. When your scooter's engine is idling, one set of fuel-delivery passages, called circuits, is being used. At part throttle openings, another set is used. When the throttle is opened fully, yet another circuit kicks in. When adjusting a carburetor, lots of valves get screwed in and out, and lots of jet combinations get tried. Each adjustment must be made individually and checked before another can be made, or it won't be clear what adjustment caused which effect. It's a time-consuming process.

In addition, fuel lines can get clogged, and they can develop leaks. Fuel pumps can stop working. Intake manifold gaskets can leak. Air filters need to be replaced. However, these problems can all be avoided through routine maintenance.

PROJECT 9
Remove Carburetor

 Time: 1 hour

 Tools: Philips-head and flat-blade screwdrivers; pliers; wrenches

 Talent: 2

 Cost: None

 Parts: None

 Benefit: Easier to clean carburetor

1

Locate the carburetor. Remove the seat, under-seat storage bin, and any body panels necessary to gain access to the carb. (See chapter 13.)

2

The carburetor should be freely accessible. Drain the gas from the float bowl. Usually this is done by locating a prominent screw on the bottom of the float bowl (the float-bowl drain screw) and loosening it until gasoline begins to pour from the float bowl.

3

Disconnect any electrical wires and vacuum hoses that are attached to the carburetor body. Electrical wires are typically for electronic choke and heating elements. Only disconnect the vacuum hoses; do not disconnect the fuel line yet. Note how the wires and hoses connect before removing them so you can reassemble everything properly.

4

Disconnect the fuel line. First, clamp the line itself so fuel doesn't leak out of the disconnected hose. Using a needle-nose pliers, release the hose clamp that secures the fuel line to the carburetor. Remove the fuel line from the carburetor with your fingers.

5 Loosen the clamp that attaches the air-intake manifold from the air cleaner to the carburetor.

6 Loosen the clamp that connects the air/fuel mixture intake manifold from the carburetor to the engine.

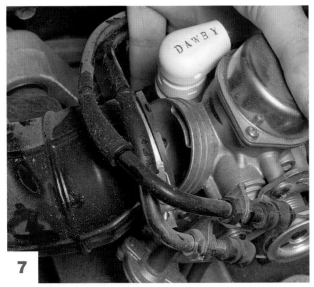

7

Separate the carburetor from the air-intake manifold (the one from the air cleaner) first, since that's the most bendable junction. This can get a bit tricky, since the system is designed to sit in a straight line with no flexible components. Push the junction between the air intake and the carburetor body apart and bend it enough to expose the carburetor opening. Then pull the carburetor opening across the air-intake opening, still pushing each component away from the other, until the carburetor is free.

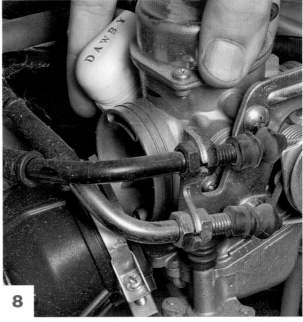

8

Sometimes the carburetor will separate from the air/fuel intake manifold (the one going into the engine) while you're wrestling with the air-intake/carburetor junction. If so, the carburetor is now sitting in your hand. If you're not so lucky, then push the air intake out of the way and pull the carburetor straight out of the air/fuel intake.

9

Remove the drain hose from the float bowl.

10 You should now be able to hold the carburetor and expose the throttle cables.

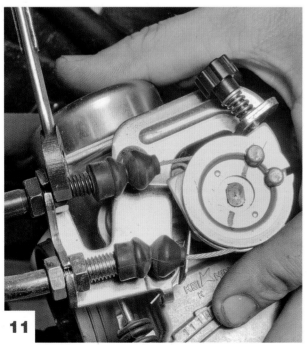

11 Remove the throttle and choke cables. First loosen the locking nuts, the ones closest to the throttle or choke assemblies. Don't turn the seating nuts, since they're the ones holding the cables in their adjusted positions.

12 Pull the cables out of the throttle and choke assemblies. The carburetor should now be completely separated from the scooter. Reassembly is the reverse order of the disassembly procedure.

PROJECT 10
Clean Carburetor

 Time: 2 hours

 Tools: Philips-head and flat-blade screwdrivers; wrenches; a supply of rags or paper towels; compressed air

★ **Talent:** 3

Cost: $

Parts: Float-bowl gasket; carburetor cleaner in a spray can

Benefit: Better running engine

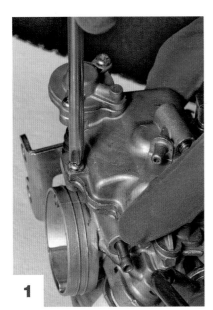

1

Remove the carburetor (see Project 9, page 62). Remove the float bowl retaining screws.

Right: Separate the float bowl from the carburetor body.

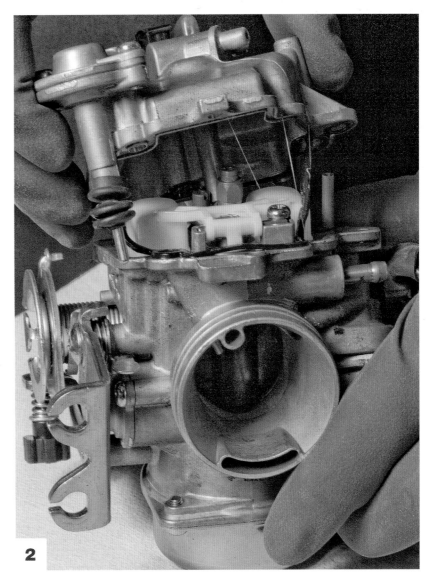

2

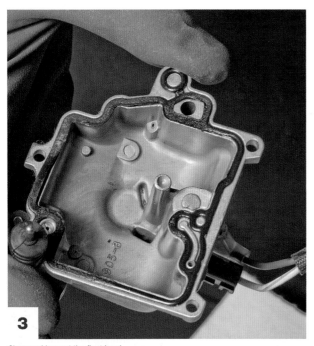

3

Clean and inspect the float bowl.

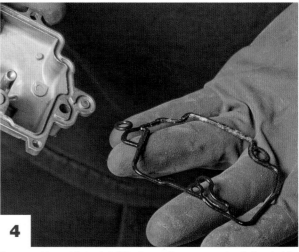

4

Remove and inspect the gasket. If it is damaged in any way, replace it. If you insist on reusing the gasket, clean it first.

5

Unscrew the pilot jet. Be very careful. Jets are made of brass, and brass is soft. It's easy to damage screwdriver slots and wrench perches on the outside surfaces of jets.

6

Remove the pilot jet and set it aside for cleaning.

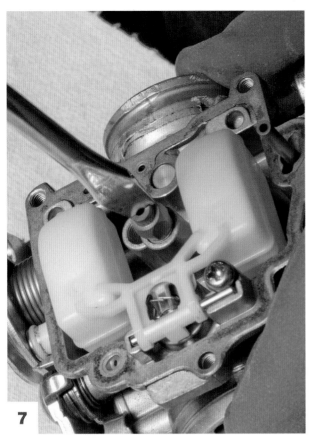

7

Unscrew and remove the main-jet/emulsion-tube assembly. Again, brass is soft, so be careful.

8

Remove the main jet/emulsion tube assembly.

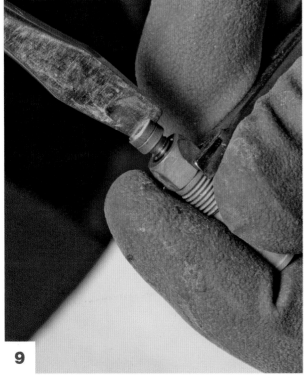

9

Unscrew the main jet from the emulsion tube.

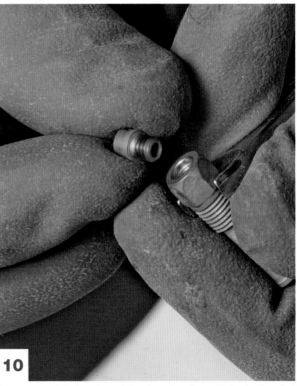

10

Separate the main jet from the emulsion tube and set them aside for cleaning.

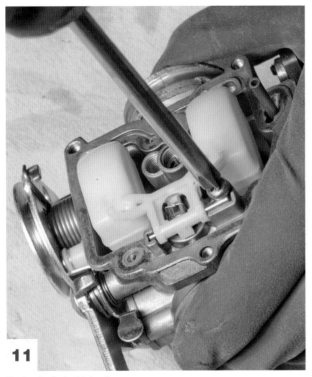

11

Remove the float retaining pin or screw.

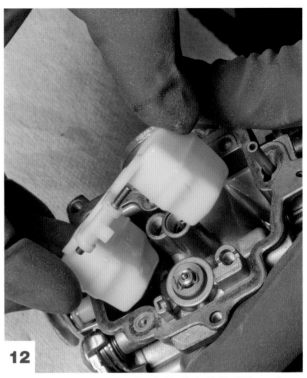

12

Remove the floats and check to see if any fuel has leaked inside. If it has, replace the whole float assembly. Otherwise just clean it.

13

Remove the seat valve. Inspect it for wear. If the sharp end has been blunted, replace the valve. If everything looks good, set it aside for cleaning.

14

Loosen and remove the diaphragm cover screws.

15

Lift off the diaphragm cover.

16

Pull off the spring.

17

Pry off the diaphragm.

18

Pull the diaphragm/slide/needle-valve assembly out of the carburetor body.

19

Inspect the diaphragm for damage, especially holes. Sometimes holes are obvious, but always hold the diaphragm up to a light to check for leaks anyway.

20

Inspect the needle and slide for wear.

21

Loosen and remove the screws holding the air/fuel mixture enrichener or choke assembly to the carburetor body.

22

Remove the enrichener or choke assembly from the carburetor body.

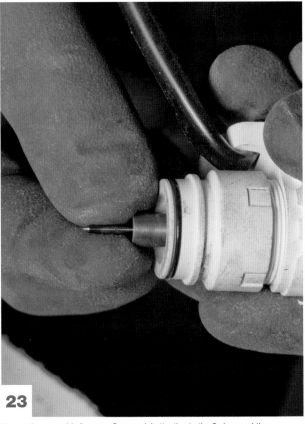

23

Inspect the assembly for wear. Pay special attention to the O-rings and the slide shaft.

24

Remove the air/fuel mixture screw. First, screw it in all the way (be careful not to seat it too hard—it's brass, and brass is soft), noting the exact number of turns (2½, 1⅜, etc.) it took to seat the screw from the position you found it in. This will be the position to which you return the air/fuel mixture screw when reassembling the carburetor. Once the screw's position has been noted, screw it out completely.

25

Remove the air/fuel mixture screw.

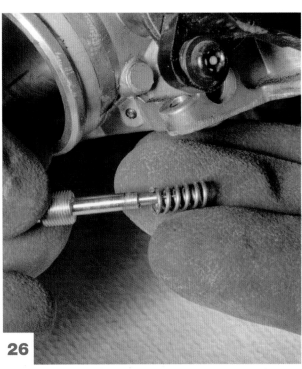

26

The air/fuel mixture screw is held in place by tension from a spring. Remove the spring from the carburetor body if it didn't come out with the screw. Put the spring back onto the screw and set both aside for cleaning.

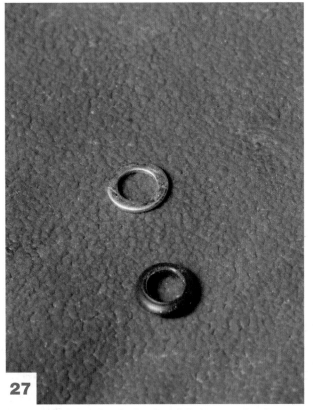

27

Remove the tiny O-ring and washer from the air/fuel mixture screw bore. Be careful not to lose them.

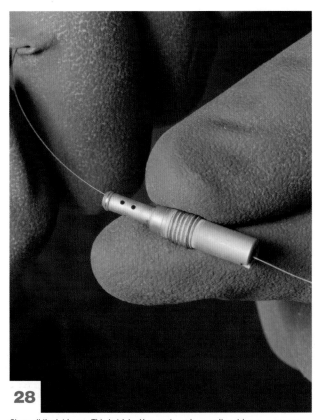

28

Clean all the jet bores. This is tricky. You can try using a guitar string as a reamer, but be careful not to scratch the inside of the soft brass bore.

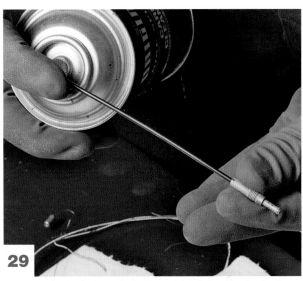

29

Your best bet for cleaning jets and other tiny parts is to just spray carburetor cleaner through the bores.

30

Dry all the jets with compressed air.

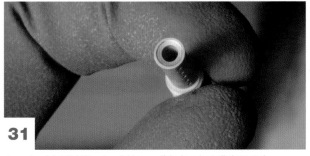

31

Inspect each jet. Hold it up to a light to see if the bore is at all obstructed.

32

Spray carburetor cleaner through each orifice in the carburetor body. These include the holes jets screw into, the point at which the enrichener/choke attaches, the air/fuel screw hole, the main venturi—if there's an opening in the carburetor body, spray carburetor cleaner through it.

33

Dry each orifice in the carburetor body with compressed air.

34

Use compressed air to dry the outside of the carburetor body.

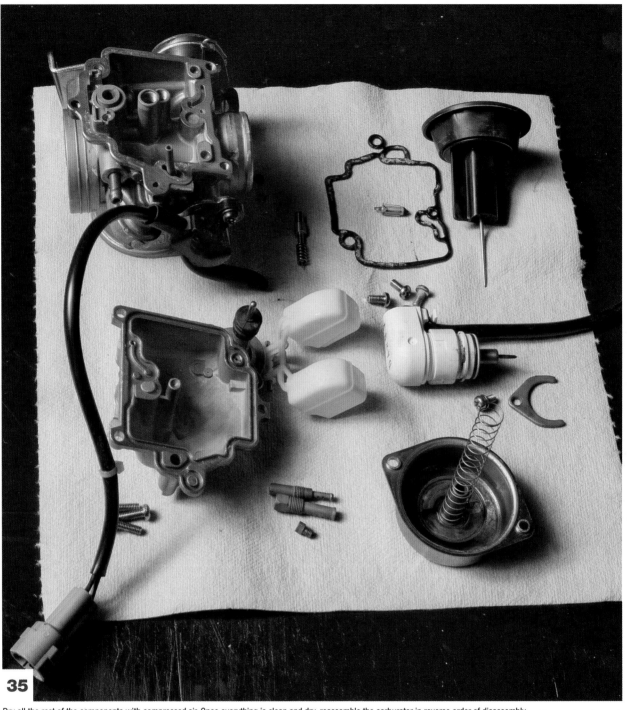

35

Dry all the rest of the components with compressed air. Once everything is clean and dry, reassemble the carburetor in reverse order of disassembly.

Chapter 6
Exhaust System

Scooter engines have to breathe. The air/fuel mixture that burns in the combustion chamber is mostly pushed in by atmospheric compression and sucked in by the vacuum created as the piston descends, but a good exhaust system will actually help pull the air/fuel mixture into the combustion chamber by pulling the spent gasses out. This means even more fuel can be burned during the firing event. More fuel burned means more power made.

HOW IT WORKS

Two principles govern this chapter: Your scooter engine makes power by burning gasoline, and everything that enters the combustion chamber exits the combustion chamber.

The combustion process is really a chemical transformation. Nothing gets destroyed, just rearranged. All the carbon molecules and all the oxygen molecules that the fuel-induction system delivers to the combustion chamber are expelled from the combustion chamber through the exhaust system. It's just that they're delivered separately and they leave together.

The combustion chamber is, essentially, a singles bar for carbon and oxygen atoms. The carburetor acts as a dating service, introducing carbon atoms (gasoline) to oxygen atoms (air) and sending them to a big dance in the combustion chamber. It gets really hot on the dance floor, the carbon and oxygen atoms hook up, then they're pushed out through the exhaust system into the real world. It's a strange metaphor, but weirdly accurate.

Although the exhaust system's function is relatively straightforward, it's more than simply a series of tubes. Two-stroke scooter engines rely on exhaust-system design to help pull exhaust gasses from the combustion chamber, and all scooter engines rely on exhaust-system components to reduce sound and harmful gas emission levels.

As the piston rises in the cylinder on its exhaust stroke, it pushes the newly formed exhaust gasses out the exhaust port into the exhaust manifold. From there they go through the header pipe, exhaust pipe, and muffler/catalytic converter until they're expelled into the atmosphere.

The header pipe is the part that's bolted to the engine. Actually, most scooter exhaust systems are single units, with the header pipe, exhaust pipe, and muffler/catalytic convertor all welded together into a continuous component. Which means that if the catalytic convertor stops changing harmful gasses into less harmful gasses, or a hole rusts through the header pipe, the whole one-piece exhaust assembly must be replaced. On the plus side, only one gasket is required to do this, between the head pipe and the engine.

STRENGTHS AND WEAKNESSES

Exhaust systems are quite simple, and most do their jobs well. They're mostly out of sight, which means they're protected from the elements. If you can hear them from more than half a block away, check for leaks at engine and header pipe connections. It's unlikely that a muffler will stop working unless it's damaged.

Of course, your muffler is pretty likely to get damaged if your scooter radically departs from the upright position. In other words, if your scooter falls over, either standing still or at speed, its muffler is probably going to take a beating. Also, the catalytic converter will eventually lose its ability to neutralize harmful exhaust gasses. And bent header and exhaust pipes restrict flow and must be replaced. Luckily, replacing exhaust systems is very simple.

PROJECT 11
Remove and Replace Exhaust System

 Time: 1 hour

 Tools: Wrenches; torque wrench and socket

 Talent: 2

 Cost: $

 Parts: Exhaust-header gasket; heat-resistant thread locker

 Benefit: Gets exhaust system out of the way for other projects; gasket replacement makes for quieter-running engine

1

Remove the air-bypass filter hose. Pinch the hose clamp and move it down the hose. *Inset:* After the clamp has been removed, carefully pull the hose from the outlet on the exhaust pipe.

2

Exhaust systems get very hot when the engine is running. Give the exhaust system time to cool before beginning this project. To remove the exhaust system, first remove the exhaust manifold header mounting bolts.

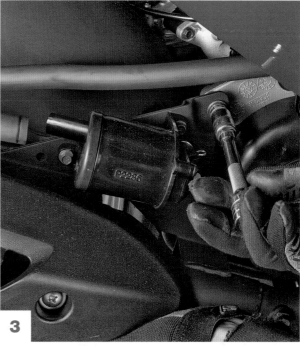

3

Remove the muffler mounting bolts. Support the muffler system as you remove the last bolt, or it will fall to the ground.

4

Remove the exhaust system from the scooter.

5

To reinstall the exhaust system, first install a new exhaust gasket. Do not reuse the old exhaust gasket. It is designed to crush into place as the exhaust header mounting bolts are tightened to their torque value. Once it has been crushed, it is cannot be loosened and recrushed.

Reinstall the muffler mounting bolts. Tighten them evenly, then torque to the torque values specified in your scooter owner's or service manual.

6

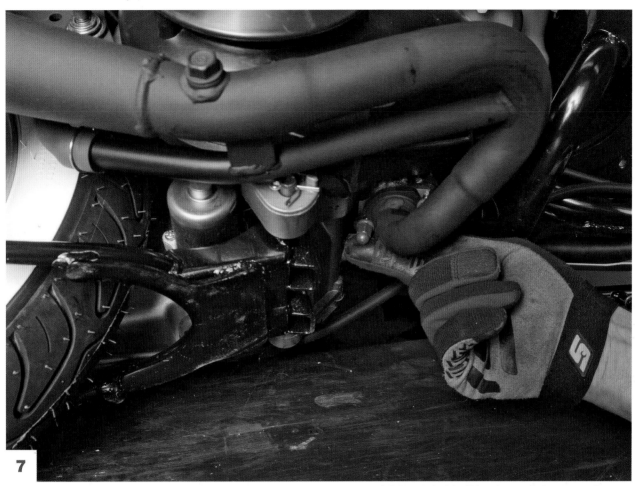

7

Reinstall the exhaust manifold header mounting bolts. Apply heat-resistant thread locker to the threads of all the mounting bolts. Tighten them evenly, then torque to the torque values specified in your scooter owner's or service manual.

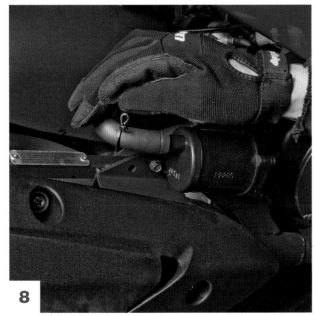

8

Reinstall the air-bypass hose.

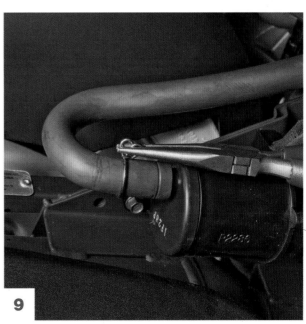

9

Pinch the hose clamp and move it back into position.

Chapter 7
Electrical System (Engine)

The battery is the core of your scooter's electrical system. Everything runs through it. Keep your battery charged and full of electrolyte, and your spark plug will always spark, your headlight will always light, and your cooling fan will always cool.

HOW IT WORKS

As discussed earlier, your scooter's engine needs three things in order to run: fuel, spark, and compression. This chapter is about the "spark" component.

The charging system is the root of the electrical system. The alternator creates electrical energy, and the battery stores it. The battery also serves as the power source for your scooter's electrical system. Everything runs through the battery. It provides power to the starter motor when you turn the key or push the starter button; it sends electricity to the coil when you push the kick starter. When the engine is running, the battery sends power to the engine control unit (ECU). When the engine gets hot, the battery provides power to the cooling fan. It is essential that the battery be in good working order for your scooter to run.

STRENGTHS AND WEAKNESSES

Over time, batteries wear out. They rely on a chemical reaction that takes place when plates of lead are bathed in an electrolyte of diluted sulfuric acid. It's a reversible reaction, which means that it goes one way when the battery is providing power, then back again when the battery is being recharged. Eventually, the plates and electrolyte lose their ability to perform the chemical reaction. A battery is deemed to be at the end of its lifecycle when it falls below about 80 percent of its rated capacity.

Nominally a 12-volt system, your scooter's battery is actually about 12.5 volts. Voltage is the battery's overall ability to do work. The battery will also be rated at some number of amps, usually between 40 and 100. This is the available current, or the amount of work the battery can do in a given amount of time. The battery's total power is its voltage multiplied by its amperage.

Think of a reservoir of water, which is to be let out in increments in order to turn a paddle wheel attached to a wheat mill. The total volume of water in the reservoir is the voltage. This is the potential to do work, in this case to grind wheat. In order to perform the work, water must be drawn from the reservoir. This is the amperage. A big opening will let a large amount of water out, and a large amount of water can turn a large paddle wheel, and a large wheel can do a lot of grinding at once. A small opening will let out less water, thus it will only be able to turn a smaller paddle wheel, which can only do a smaller amount of grinding. In other words, the more amps your battery has (the larger the opening in your reservoir), the more work your battery can perform (the more wheat you can grind at once).

Even when your scooter is just sitting unused, the battery discharges at a certain rate. Of course, using your scooter will discharge the battery even more. As the battery discharges, your scooter's alternator recharges it. To do this, the alternator should provide a current of between 13 and 14 amps. This is enough to run the scooter while at the same time providing enough excess power to recharge the battery.

It is possible for an engine to run with a discharged battery. In fact, if your battery is dead and you can get your scooter started, riding it at speed for half an hour or so should recharge the battery sufficiently. You need to keep the engine revs up; idling in traffic will not do the job.

CHARGING SYSTEM

The alternator is the heart of the charging system. It spins at the end of the crankshaft, either from being mounted directly to it or via belts or gears. As it spins, it creates an electrical current. The amount of current the alternator creates is tied to how fast it spins. Thus at low revs, it creates less than it does at high revs. This is why the alternator won't recharge a dead battery by idling in traffic. It must spin fast enough to create more current than is needed to simply keep the scooter running.

At high revs, the alternator can create more than 15 amps. Left unattended, this would fry your scooter's electrical system. Thus, a regulator is built into the alternator to keep it from producing more than about 14.5 amps.

There are two types of electrical current: alternating current (AC) and direct current (DC). Your house runs on AC. Your scooter runs on DC. Your scooter's alternator creates AC electricity, however. A series of diodes and other switches convert it to DC.

If the alternator is the heart of the charging system, the battery is its focus. A battery that is old or defective won't take a charge. It might momentarily take the alternator's current and pass it on to the rest of your scooter's electrical system, allowing the scooter to run, but it won't retain a charge. Once you turn off your scooter, it won't just restart.

To determine whether electrical problems reside in the battery or the alternator, use a voltmeter to measure the battery at its terminals with the scooter engine off. It should be about 12.5 volts. If it's not, the battery is faulty. With the scooter running, it should be between 13 and 14 volts. If it's not, the alternator is faulty.

Of course, there could be other problems, like a short circuit or a blown fuse. Fuses are easy to check. Short circuits are harder, but not impossible. Just start at the beginning of the system and work toward the end, measuring current. As soon as you find a spot where there is no current, you've found your fault.

IGNITION SYSTEM

The most important function of the electrical system is to provide spark to the engine. This is done through the ignition system.

Most modern scooters have electronic ignitions. These are basically computers that send electrical pulses to the spark plug, via the coil, at properly timed intervals. There are no adjustments to be made. If the plug isn't getting spark, and the high-tension wire to the plug is good, and the coil is good, then the ECU might be bad. If this is the case, it must be replaced. ECU failure is rare, however. More often it's the coil or plug wire that must be replaced—or, of course, the plug itself.

STARTING SYSTEM

If your scooter has an electric starter, (and virtually all scooters made today have electric starters), the starter system consists of an electric starter motor that spins the engine to get it started, a solenoid to move the starter motor gear onto the flywheel so it can turn the engine, a relay switch to provide electrical current to the starter motor and solenoid to give it power, and an ignition switch to provide current to the relay. There's also a fuse in the system to protect it. The ignition switch usually involves a key, either to turn the system on or to provide power, so another switch, usually a push-button, can turn it on.

As with the other electrical systems, faults can be traced with a trouble light or a meter. If the starter motor isn't getting current, check the solenoid. If the solenoid isn't getting power, check the relay. If the relay isn't getting power, check the ignition switch. And, of course, check the wiring between components.

COOLING SYSTEM

Whether liquid- or air-cooled, your scooter probably has a cooling fan. It is controlled by a temperature sensor. When the sensor tells it to, a switch turns on the fan motor. There is usually a relay switch in the system, too, as well as a fuse. As with all electrical system faults, cooling fan malfunctions can be traced with a meter or a trouble light.

PROJECT 12
Remove, Check, and Replace Fuse

Time: 1/2 hour

Tools: Fuse puller

Talent: 1

Cost: $

Parts: Fuse(s)

Benefit: A working electrical system

1

Locate the fusebox. There might be more than one. Fuseboxes can be located inside storage compartments, under the seat, or behind easily removable body trim panels. Consult your owner's manual for locations. Open the panel or remove body panels as necessary. (See chapter 13.)

3

Remove the fuse. A fuse puller is handy for this step but not necessary.

2

Remove the fusebox cover.

4

Check the fuse. Blown fuses are easily determined by the evidence of the fuse having burned. Besides residue from the burn, the filament inside the fuse will be not be continuous from one end to the other. If the fuse is blown, replace the fuse. Replace the fusebox cover.

PROJECT 13
Remove, Check, and Replace Battery

Time: 1 hour

Tools: Wrenches; voltmeter; battery tester; emery cloth

Talent: 1

Cost: $$

Parts: Battery

Benefit: A scooter that starts

1

Locate the battery. The battery is usually behind a body panel. Consult your owner's manual for the exact location. Remove the battery cover (see project 31, page 149). Remove the battery cables. Remove the negative cable first. This is the one attached to the battery terminal that has a "–" sign next to it. The negative cable is usually all black and is a much simpler assembly than the positive cable. It can be traced to a ground point on the chassis. Loosen the screw and remove it, being careful not to let the wrench contact any metal parts of the scooter.

2

Remove the positive battery cable. This is the one attached to the battery terminal with the "+" sign next to it. The positive cable usually has a red casing at the end and might have a number of smaller wires combined with one big one. Loosen the screw and remove it, being careful not to let the wrench contact any metal parts of the scooter.

3

Move the cables out of the way.

4

Lift the battery out of its compartment.

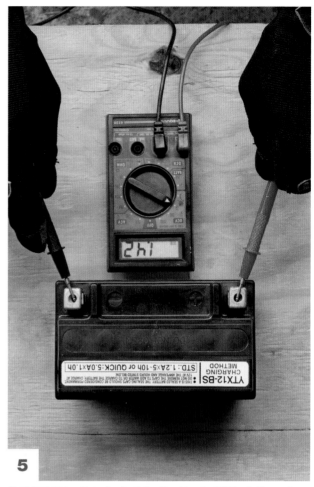

5

Check the battery with a voltmeter. It should register about 13.1 volts. Too much less or more and the battery should be replaced.

Use a battery tester to see if the battery accepts a charge. If it doesn't, it should be replaced.

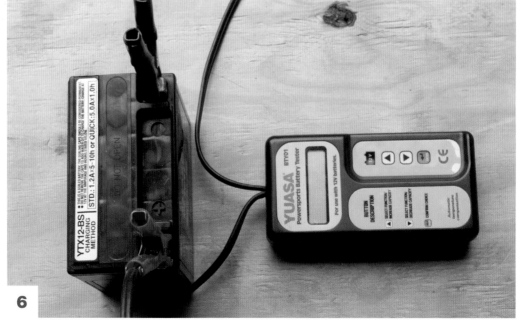

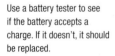

6

Before reinstalling the battery, use emery cloth to clean the battery terminals.

7

8

Next, use emery cloth to clean the cable connections itself.

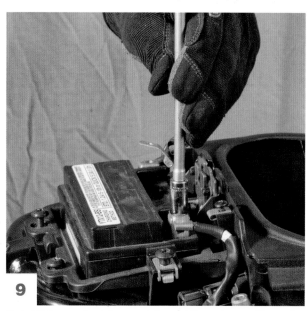

9

The installation procedure is the reverse of removal. Be sure to connect the negative cable after the positive cable has been connected. Also, make sure the wrench doesn't contact any metal parts of the scooter when you're tightening the battery cable bolts.

Chapter 8
Transmission and Final Drive

Outer drive-belt covers just add weight. And how cool would it be to watch the variator and clutch do their jobs? Mean-looking as this is, though, it's really dangerous (your pants cuff could get pulled into a pulley) and not very conducive to long drive-belt component lives (sand, grit, and pants cuffs in the system will hasten its demise).

HOW IT WORKS

While decades ago scooters came with shiftable gears, most modern scooters are equipped with constantly variable transmissions. The constantly variable transmission (CVT) relies on a variator (sometimes called a torque converter) to convert engine speed to belt speed, a belt to transmit engine power to the clutch, a clutch to engage the gearbox, and a gearbox to turn the rear-wheel axle.

The beauty of the system is that, unlike the automatic transmissions in a car, engine speed isn't necessarily linked to road speed. In other words, engine rpm can crank up to a level governed by the twist grip, then the variator and clutch kick in, setting the scooter in motion and regulating how fast it travels while the engine maintains a more or less constant rpm level.

All components can be worked on while installed on the scooter.

The variator is attached to the engine's crankshaft. It is basically the pulley that drives the drive belt, although it is more accurately a pulley split into two halves that drives the drive belt. While a normal pulley of a fixed size would have only one place for the drive belt to go, this pulley has two angled surfaces on which the belt runs.

Both the inner and outer halves of the pulley are fixed onto the crankshaft, but the inner half can slide outward along the shaft, away from the engine, and back inward. This effectively changes the size of the drive belt's driven pulley. As engine rpm increases, a series of weights are pushed by centrifugal force onto angled plates that force the inner half of the pulley outward, away from the engine, increasing the size of the pulley. As engine rpm decreases, the weights release their force on the angled plates, allowing the belt itself to force the two halves of the pulleys apart, decreasing the size of the pulley.

The heavier the weights, the quicker centrifugal force will push the two halves of the pulley together or grow larger. If the weights are too heavy, acceleration can suffer, as the engine is made to work harder than it otherwise would because of the higher effective gearing.

Think of a bicycle with multiple chain rings to choose from up front. The smaller the chain ring, the slower the bicycle's speed, and the easier it is to accelerate. The bigger the chain ring, the higher the bicycle's speed, and the harder it is to accelerate. When the pulley halves are as far apart as they can go, it's like having a small pulley. When they are forced all the way together, it's like having a big pulley. Between the two extremes are an infinite number of pulley sizes.

CLUTCH

The clutch is attached to the gearbox input shaft, which transmits drive to the gearbox, which makes the rear wheel turn. Like the variator, the clutch is also an angle-walled pulley split into two halves, one of which slides in and out to effectively create larger and smaller pulleys. In this case, it is the outer half that slides in and out.

Unlike the variator, however, the two halves of the clutch pulley are pushed apart by the belt itself and pulled back together by a spring, called the contra spring. As higher engine rpm forces the variator pulley halves together up front (making the driving pulley bigger), the belt, being a fixed length, has no choice but to force the clutch pulley halves apart (making the driven pulley smaller). When engine rpm is low, the variator pulley gets effectively smaller, and the clutch spring forces the clutch pulley halves back together, creating a larger pulley.

If the contra spring isn't strong enough, the belt will overcome the spring and force the pulley halves apart, even at low rpm. This creates the effect of being in too high a gear. If a scooter accelerates well but bogs when it tries to go up a hill, the clutch likely needs a stronger contra spring.

Again, think of a bicycle, but this time think of the derailleur and gear cluster out back. The bigger the sprocket used, the slower the speeds and the better the acceleration; the smaller the sprocket, the higher the speeds and the harder the acceleration.

DRIVE BELT

Drive belts are typically made of rubber with embedded cords to add strength. Better belts use Kevlar cords. Some belts have teeth on both sides, others just have teeth on one side (the inner side).

A typical belt identification code might be HTD-500-5M-15. HTD stands for high-tension drive; 500 refers to the belt's length in centimeters; 5 refers to the space between the teeth in centimeters; and 15 refers to its width in centimeters.

A scooter's drive belt is typically quite strong, but with the variator and clutch continually pressing on its sides, it will wear out. Usually it just gets worn until it's too narrow, but occasionally a belt will develop cracks from age. This generally happens when a scooter racks up more years than miles. A cracked belt can disintegrate at any given moment, causing much trauma inside the belt cover.

GEARBOX

Unlike the transmission on a motorcycle or car, a scooter's gearbox isn't used to vary engine speed versus road speed. It merely transmits to the rear wheel the torque applied by the belt to the clutch pulley.

There are three shafts in the gearbox: input, intermediate, and output. As noted above, the clutch is attached to one end of the input shaft; at the other end of the input shaft is a pinion gear. It meshes with a smaller pinion gear on the intermediate shaft. A second, larger gear on the intermediate shaft meshes with a gear on the outside end of the output shaft, which drives the rear wheel.

Each shaft is supported by bearings, and each shaft has an oil seal. Be careful not to damage or lose these should you disassemble the gearbox.

Ever since Piaggio produced the first Vespa scooter in 1946, most scooters have transmissions that are part of the rear swingarm (which, technically speaking, wasn't a "swingarm" on the first Vespa since that early machine had no rear suspension and said arm did very little swinging).

Ian Paterson/Alamy

PROJECT 14
Remove and Replace Drive-Belt Cover

 Time: 1 hour

 Tools: Wrenches; torque wrench and socket; dead-blow hammer or rubber mallet

 Talent: 2

 Cost: $

 Parts: Drive-belt cover gasket

 Benefit: Allows access to drive belt, clutch, and variator

1 Remove the body panels as necessary. (See chapter 13.) Remove the brake cable or hydraulic line brackets from the transmission (if necessary).

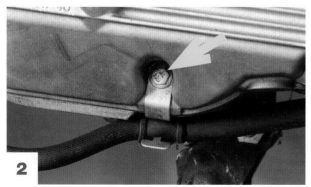

2 Locate the bracket.

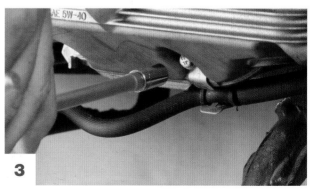

3 Remove the bolt that holds the bracket in place.

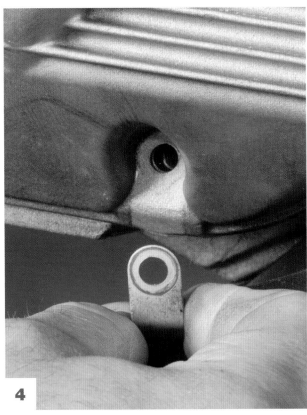

4

Move the bracket out of the way. Repeat as necessary.

5

Detach the air-cooling duct (if necessary). First, locate the duct.

6

Remove or loosen the clamp securing the bracket into place and detach the bracket.

7

Remove the oil filler plug (if necessary).

8

Remove kick-start lever. Using a small prybar or screwdriver, remove the plastic trim on the belt cover (if necessary).

9

Remove the airbox cover and any other pieces that might be in the way of removing the drive-belt cover itself.

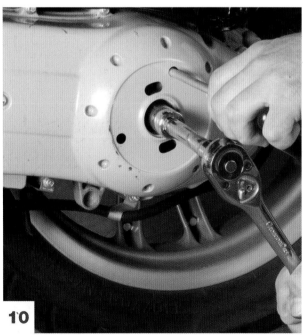

10

Remove the nut on the outer end of the gearbox input shaft. Unscrew the nut with a proper wrench. Use a clutch-locking tool, or insert a Phillips screwdriver through the hole in drive-belt cover and the hole in the clutch cover behind the drive-belt cover in order to lock the clutch in place so it doesn't spin when turning the nut on the outer end of the gearbox input shaft.

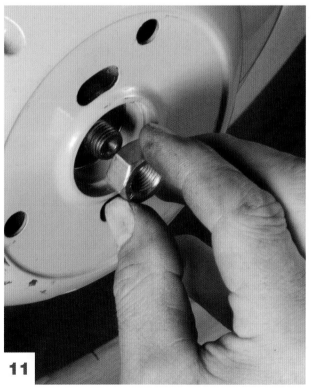

11

Remove the nut and washer.

12 Remove the bolts fixing the drive-belt cover in place. Loosen first in a crisscross pattern around the edge, then loosen any bolts in the center.

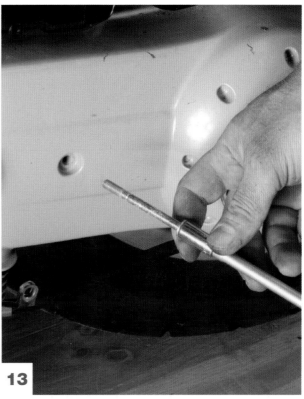

13 After the bolts have been loosened in the proper order, remove them from the belt cover. Note the position of each bolt; some might be longer than others and must be replaced in the exact same holes from which they were removed.

14 Remove the drive-belt cover. It might be necessary to use a rubber mallet or a dead-blow hammer to rap the cover a few times in order to break it free. If such a hammer is not available, you can use a block of wood to absorb the shock from rapping the cover with a normal hammer.

15 After rapping with a hammer, use a pry bar to further separate the cover from the drive-belt case.

16

Once the cover is loose, it might be necessary to maneuver the cover around such things as the oil-filler tube and passenger footrest. This can make the procedure a bit tricky, but with some perseverance the cover will come off. When it does, make note of any positioning dowels and clips in order to properly replace the cover when the time comes.

17

Inspect the gasket (if there is one). Replace the gasket if it is at all damaged. Note the position of the gearbox input shaft spacer (if necessary). To ease reassembly, note how the kick starter engages (if necessary). Inspect the mating surface of the cover.

18

Inspect the inside of the cover and the drive-belt case. There will be some black residue from normal drive-belt wear; if the residue seems excessive and the drive belt seems overly worn for the amount of time it's been in service, there might be a problem with the variator or clutch that needs to be addressed. Clean the residue from the inside of the cover and drive-belt case with solvent; be careful not to get any solvent on the variator or clutch pulleys or the belt itself. To replace the drive-belt cover, reverse the removal procedure. Apply a small amount of grease to the bolt threads. Note the placement of the positioning dowels or clips. Note the kick-start lever placement; before tightening the cover into place, check to see if the kick-start lever engages. Finger tighten the bolts, then tighten the bolts to their proper torque in a crisscross pattern.

PROJECT 15
Remove, Inspect, and Replace Drive Belt

 Time: 1 hour

 Tools: Wrenches; impact wrench and sockets

 Talent: 2

 Cost: $$

Parts: Drive belt

Benefit: A scooter that gets you from point A to point B

1

Remove the drive-belt cover. (See Project 14, page 90) Loosen the variator center nut. To do this, the variator must be kept from turning. Special holding tools are available for this. An alternative method is to use an impact wrench. *Inset:* Remove the variator center nut. Some scooter manufacturers recommend replacing this nut when reassembling; check this with your dealer.

2

Remove the outer cover (if necessary).

3

Remove the outer half of the variator pulley.

4

Remove the clutch shaft spacer. Be careful not to lose any of the washers that come out with it; note the order and direction of the washers.

5

Pull out the clutch drum assembly. It is not necessary to remove the clutch assembly, just pull it out enough to enable the belt to clear the gearbox housing.

6 Pull the top and bottom of the belt back as far as it will go.

7 Lift the belt around the clutch drum assembly and off the variator shaft. Inspect the belt for cracks and wear. Use a caliper to measure the belt's width. Replace the belt if there are any cracks, strange wear patterns, or if it measures too narrow. Reverse the procedures above to reinstall the belt.

SECTION 3
CHASSIS AND BODY

Scooters are the most entertaining two-wheeled devices ever made, but they are still members of the motorcycle family, and as such, they share all the same consequences. Because most scooters have small tires with little gyroscopic stability and extremely small contact patches, they are even more susceptible to chassis and suspension failures than motorcycles. Therefore, it is even more important to keep these systems in tip-top shape. To get at the chassis and suspension components—or any other component on a scooter (especially a modern scooter)— you'll first have to remove some bodywork.

Chassis Troubleshooting Guide

PROBLEM	PROBABLE CAUSES	ACTION TO REPAIR
Front end noise/vibration	Loose, worn, or damaged steering-head bearing	Replace/repack/adjust steering-head bearing
	Loose front axle nut	Retorque front axle nut
	Loose or faulty front shock (Arm-type suspension)	Retorque/replace front shock
	Bent fork tube	Replace fork tube
	Warped front brake disc	Replace disc
	Loose or faulty front-wheel bearing	Repack/adjust/replace front-wheel bearing
	Front wheel out of balance	Balance front wheel
	Faulty front tire	Replace tire
Rear-end noise or vibration	Loose or faulty rear shock absorber	Retorque/replace rear shock absorber
	Loose/worn swingarm/shock linkage	Adjust/repack/replace swingarm bearing and shock linkage
	Warped rear brake disc	Replace rear brake disc
	Loose or faulty front-wheel bearing	
	Repack/adjust/replace rear-wheel bearing	
	Rear wheel out of balance	Balance rear wheel
	Faulty rear tire	Replace tire
Handlebars hard to turn	Steering-head bearings too tight	Repack/adjust steering-head bearings
	Faulty steering-head bearings/races	Replace steering-head bearings
	Bent steering stem	Replace steering stem
	Front tire pressure too low	Check and adjust tire pressure
Scooter tracks poorly, wanders	Faulty rear-wheel bearing	Repack/adjust/replace rear-wheel bearing
	Front or rear tire pressure too low	Check and adjust tire pressure
Scooter wobbles more than normal	Faulty front-wheel bearing	Repack/adjust/replace front-wheel bearing
Scooter pulls to one side	Wheels not aligned	Check/adjust wheel alignment
	Bent fork tube	Replace fork tube
	Bent steering stem	Replace steering stem
	Bent frame	Replace frame
Suspension too hard	Incorrect viscosity/too much fork fluid	Change fork fluid
	Fork springs too hard	Change fork springs
	Shock spring too hard	Change shock spring
		Replace shock absorber
	Bent fork tube	Replace fork tube
	Bent shock-absorber shaft	Replace shock absorber
	Front or rear tire pressure too high	Check and adjust tire pressure
Suspension too soft	Incorrect viscosity or too little fork fluid	Change fluid
	Fork springs too soft	Change fork springs
	Shock spring too soft	Change shock spring
		Replace shock absorber
	Front or rear tire pressure too low	Check and adjust tire pressure
Suspension leaks	Faulty fork seals	Replace fork seals
	Faulty shock seals	Replace shock
Brakes squeak or grind	Worn or dirty brake pads	Clean or replace brake pads
	Brake shoes out of adjustment	Adjust brake cable
	Worn or dirty brake shoes	Clean or replace brake shoes
Poor braking performance	Brake cable out of adjustment	Adjust brake cable
	Worn or incorrect brake pads	Replace brake pads
	Worn or incorrect brake shoes	Replace brake shoes

PROBLEM	PROBABLE CAUSES	ACTION TO REPAIR
Brake pads wear unevenly	Faulty brake disc Faulty drum	Replace brake disc Replace brake drum
Brakes drag	Sticky caliper Brake shoes out of adjustment	Rebuild caliper Adjust brake cable
Speedometer doesn't work	Broken speedometer cable	Check and replace speedometer cable

Body Electrical Troubleshooting Guide

PROBLEM	PROBABLE CAUSES	ACTION TO REPAIR
Headlight doesn't work	Fuse blown Bulb burned out Faulty handlebar switch Faulty wiring	Check and replace fuse Replace bulb Check and replace handlebar switch Check/repair/replace wiring harness
Brake or taillight doesn't work	Fuse blown Bulb burned out Faulty brake-light switch Faulty wiring	Check and replace fuse Replace bulb Check and replace brake-light switches Check/repair/replace wiring harness
Turn-signal light doesn't work	Fuse blown Bulb burned out Faulty handlebar switch Faulty turn-signal relay Faulty wiring	Check and replace fuse Replace bulb Check and replace handlebar switch Check and replace turn-signal relay Check/repair/replace wiring harness
License plate light doesn't work	Fuse blown Bulb burned out Faulty wiring	Check and replace fuse Replace bulb Check/repair/replace wiring harness
Instrument panel light doesn't work	Bulb burned out Faulty wiring	Replace bulb Check/repair/replace wiring harness
Oil warning light doesn't work	Bulb burned out Faulty wiring Faulty oil light diode	Replace bulb Check/repair/replace wiring harness Check/replace oil warning light diode
Horn doesn't work	Fuse blown Bulb burned out Faulty handlebar switch Faulty wiring Faulty horn	Check and replace fuse Replace bulb Check and replace handlebar switch Check/repair/replace wiring harness Check and replace horn

Chapter 9
Frame

You don't normally see a scooter's frame. Kind of a pity, really.

HOW IT WORKS

Your scooter is a collection of components. It's an engine and drivetrain, suspension, wheels and brakes, body parts, seat, and handlebars, all functioning as one single unit. This unit is defined by the frame. Each component is attached to the frame, and it is the frame that gives your scooter its composition. The frame's head tube locates the forks, handlebars, and front wheel. The swingarm locates the rear suspension and wheel. The frame positions the engine and its cooling system, and it provides mounting points for bodywork, footpegs, and the seat. The frame is your scooter's skeleton.

In very basic terms, the frame has three functions: It holds the engine, it supports the rider, and it connects the wheels to one another. Scooter frames are generally welded together out of tubular and pressed steel. Up front is the head tube, through which the steering stem passes, mounting the front forks and handlebars. The head tube is connected to the down tubes, which actually go down, then back. Toward the rear, the tubes form a cradle to hold the engine and drivetrain and to mount the seat and footpegs. The rear suspension's swingarm is supported in the front by the engine in most modern scooters. The bottom of the shock absorber is mounted to the rear of the swingarm, and the top mounts to the rear frame tubes. The rear wheel is also mounted to the rear of the swingarm.

STRENGTHS AND WEAKNESSES

For the most part, the frame needs no attention. The steering stem rotates on bearings in the steering head. These bearings are packed in grease, which will need to be periodically replenished. The swingarm also rotates on bearings packed in grease, and it will require the same care. Other than that, there is no maintenance to be performed. If the frame's paint gets nicked, touch it up so the metal doesn't rust. But, since most scooter frames are enclosed in bodywork, they are protected from dings.

If you crash your scooter, however, the frame can get bent. When this happens, straightening the frame might be possible, but most likely it will need to be replaced. This essentially means disassembling and reassembling the entire scooter. The alternatives are to ride the bent scooter or get another one. The first option is unsafe, since bent frames don't track straight and can suddenly go out of control when upset by bumps and corners. The second option is usually the easiest and cheapest.

PROJECT 16
Checking Wheel Alignment

 Time: 1 hour

 Tools: 30 feet or more of string or twine

 Talent: 1

 Cost: None

 Parts: None

 Benefit: A scooter that goes straight

On most modern scooters, the rear suspension's swingarm is actually composed mostly of the inner half of the drive-belt cover. At the front end, the inner half of the drive-belt cover is molded into the engine crankcase. At the back end, the inner half of the drive-belt cover is molded into the gearbox. This swinging arm/drive-belt-cover assembly is supported in the front by the engine mount. The bottom of the shock absorber is mounted to the rear of the swingarm, and the top of the shock absorber mounts to the rear frame tubes. The rear wheel is also mounted to the rear of the swingarm at the gearbox.

A curious effect of this design is that, as the swingarm goes up and down over bumps, the engine pivots around an axis created by the engine/swingarm mount at the front end, while the wheel and gearbox essentially go straight up and down at the back.

1

Make sure the front tire is both pointing straight and fixed in place. Attach a string to the rear of the rear tire.

2

Stretch the string through the center-stand to the front tire.

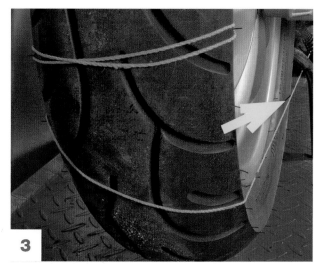

3

Move the string sideways until it just touches the front of the rear tire.

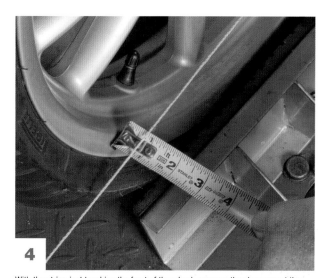

4

With the string just touching the front of the wheel, measure the clearance at the rear of the front tire.

5

With string still in place, measure the clearance at the front of the front tire. It should be the same as the clearance at the rear of the front tire. If it is different, the wheels are not aligned. Have a dealer or repair shop check the frame and forks to see if either is bent.

Chapter 10
Suspension System

Scooters are already quick, but they're not generally very precise handlers. With the right suspension, scooters can be nimble too.

HOW IT WORKS

The wheels ride over road surfaces, and road surfaces have imperfections. Whether a pothole or a sudden rise, these imperfections are transmitted to the scooter and its rider. The suspension's job is to absorb as much of this transmission as possible.

In the most simple terms, the suspension allows the scooter to sort of float above the wheels. As the wheels encounter road surface changes, the wheel reacts by going up or down. The suspension allows the wheel to go up and down without making the frame follow, or at least not follow so drastically.

Scooter suspensions come in a wide variety of configurations, but they all function in essentially the same

manner. Basically, springs connect the wheels to the frame. But, left unattended, these springs would not only transmit to the frame every change in road surface encountered by the wheels, they'd continue to mimic those changes in weaker and weaker oscillations until all the energy was dissipated. So the springs' movement is damped. This is accomplished through hydraulics. As the suspension compresses, pistons inside the forks and shocks are made to push through hydraulic fluid, displacing it. A complex series of passages inside the fork and shock bodies are employed to control the movement of the hydraulic fluid. The ultimate goal is to allow the spring to compress and then rebound to its static position without further oscillations. Worn-out shocks are easily visible because they continue to go up and down after

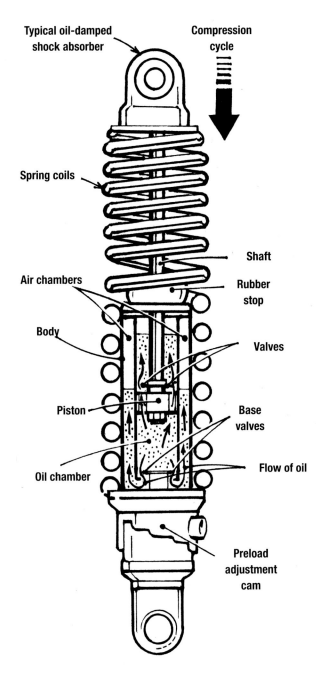

Typical oil-damped shock absorber

Compression cycle

Spring coils

Air chambers

Body

Piston

Oil chamber

Shaft

Rubber stop

Valves

Base valves

Flow of oil

Preload adjustment cam

Shock absorber

an initial jolt. Telescopic forks don't wear out, but the fluid inside them does and must be periodically replaced.

Up front, forks can be telescopic or monolever with a leading or trailing link. Telescopic forks are self-contained, rebuildable units; monolever designs employ a coilover shock absorber, which can be rebuilt or replaced. The monolever itself rotates on bushings. These bushings will need periodic replacement.

At the back of a scooter, the frame is suspended over the swingarm by one or two coilover shock absorbers. Single-shock designs use bigger components, while twin-shock arrangements use smaller ones. Both types are effective, but single-shock systems are, obviously, less complex. In any case, the rear suspension supports quite a bit of the overall load, what with the rider and engine both being nearby.

STRENGTHS AND WEAKNESSES

As with all scooter components, suspension design has been refined to the point where handling is quite predictable. Unless you hit a giant pothole, your scooter's suspension should be able to cope with whatever the road surface throws at it. And since most designs rely on self-contained spring-and-shock-absorber assemblies, when one unit wears out, it can easily be swapped for a new part. Plus, fork fluid comes in a variety of viscosities. Thicker fluid can be substituted for thinner fluid, and vice versa, in order to fine-tune the forks. Fork and shock-absorber springs can be changed from either less resistant to more resistant or more resistant to less resistant.

But suspension systems require moving parts. Not only that, but many of those moving parts are inside closed, pressurized hydraulic subsystems. So there are a lot of gaskets and seals involved, which can eventually leak. When, say, a shock absorber leaks, it causes more than a stain. The volume of hydraulic fluid inside is depleted, destroying the unit's ability to absorb energy from the spring. Wallowing, bouncing scooters are dangerous. And they're not much fun to ride.

The tricky part is being able to realize when your suspension components need attention. Sometimes they blow out in one swell foop, but normally they just wear out over time. It's hard to notice gradual degradation. Check suspension components regularly—and objectively.

PROJECT 17
Checking and Replacing Suspension Components

 Time: 1/4–2 hours

 Tools: Wrenches; torque wrench and socket

 Talent: 3

 Cost: None–$$$

 Parts: Shock absorber; front forks

 Benefit: A better-handling scooter

If your scooter feels wallowy, bouncy, or imprecise when you ride it, chances are one or more of the hydraulic suspension components is shot. Forks and shock absorbers work by compressing fluid through orifices. When your scooter hits a bump and compresses the suspension component, pressure is applied to this fluid. If not for strategically placed rubber seals, every time you hit a bump, fluid would spray out of your scooter's forks and shock absorbers. The rubber seals that prevent this can be replaced in motorcycle forks and shock, but the suspension components that come on today's scooters are disposable items. Since you can't rebuild them, the only alternative is to replace them.

Start by making a visual inspection of the component. For shock absorbers, look inside the spring at the shaft where it enters the shock absorber body. It should be clean and dry. The section of the shaft that slides into the shock body, or of the fork tube that slides into the fork slider, will probably be noticeably cleaner than the rest of it. This is because the rubber seal in the shock body or fork slider is sliding along the surface of the shaft or fork tube—which is why it's best to keep your scooter clean, so dirt doesn't wreck the rubber seals as they do their job.

1

2

We'll use a fork for our example because it's easier to photograph, but the situations are the same for forks and shock absorbers. If there is gunk or oil present on the shock shaft or fork tube, the seal is leaking. Also note the accumulation of sludge where the shaft or tube enters the shock body or fork slider.

3

If you find that you need to replace one or more suspension components, now might be a good time to upgrade. Suspension component upgrades add far more enjoyment per dollar than engine modifications, and they're much easier to perform. For example, swapping shock absorbers involves only two bolts per shock.

4

Start by locating the upper and lower shock-absorber mounting bolts.

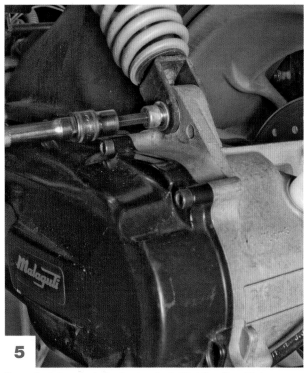

5

Remove the bottom shock-absorber mounting bolt first. Sometimes this is a through-bolt, other times it's simply a bolt that screws into a threaded hole cast into the swingarm. If it's a through bolt, you'll need to hold the nut while you turn the bolt. If not, you can just use one wrench. First, loosen the bolt.

6

Before removing the bolt, be sure that the back end of the engine/swingarm/drive-belt housing/drivebox assembly is supported, or it will be very hard to pull the bolt out, and the swingarm assembly will fall as soon as the bolt is removed. After the bolt is out, set the rear tire down onto the ground.

7

Loosen the upper mounting bolt. Again, this might be a through-bolt with a nut, or it might be a single bolt that threads into a hole molded into the frame.

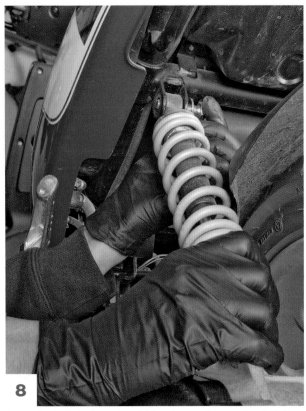

8

Support the shock absorber so it won't fall, and remove the upper mounting bolt.

9

Remove the shock.

10

Put the new shock into place.

11

Install the top mounting bolt. Tighten it, but not to its specified torque value yet.

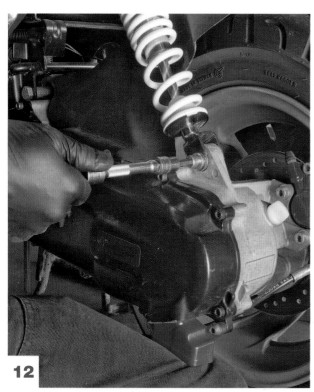

12

Install the bottom mounting bolt. Note how you can use your knee to support the rear end of the swingarm in order to get it into place. Tighten the bolt, but not to its specified torque value yet.

13

Tighten the upper and lower mounting bolts to their specified torque value (check your scooter's service manual).

Chapter 11
Wheels and Tires

No matter how well you maintain your scooter, sometimes ya gotta improvise.

HOW IT WORKS

This is where the rubber meets the road. Literally. Of course, we'll never know how the wheel was invented, but it probably involved an observant caveman and a happy accident with a big, round rock or a long, straight log. The concept's been continually refined since, and today your scooter rolls on the culmination of all that research and development.

Soft, rubber tires inflated with air and mounted on aluminum rims that rotate around axles on bearings: The concept behind the wheel is quite simple to begin with, but grows increasingly complex the faster it's made to turn. A wheelbarrow tire doesn't need to inflate, and its rim doesn't need to ride on axle bearings. Your scooter, on the other hand, needs both these things and more. Not only must its tires inflate, but they must be uniformly round and balanced. Not only must its rims be uniformly round and balanced, they must ride on axle bearings. Precisely manufactured and properly adjusted axle bearings, riding in a bed of grease thick enough to provide protection at high speeds and temperatures, yet thin enough to allow the wheel assembly to rotate freely.

All sorts of mathematically describable principles are invoked, from inertia and friction to gyroscopic action and the way rubber heats up as it's made to flex. If there's a place in the tire where the rubber is thicker than it is at similar points around the circumference, if the rim is even slightly egg-shaped or bent, if there's too much space between the bearings and the cup and race that hold them, then your scooter's wheel will bounce up and down, oscillate from side to side, and vibrate along a range from annoying to dangerous. The larger the wheel's diameter, the harder it is to knock over, thus the more stable it will be. A less inflated tire gives a softer ride, but offers more rolling resistance and wears out faster.

STRENGTHS AND WEAKNESSES

The tire is basically a carcass of fibers encased in rubber. The fibers are oriented either perpendicular to the direction of travel (radial ply) or a combination of parallel and roughly 45-degree angles to the direction of travel (bias ply). The rubber must be soft enough to grip the road surface, yet hard enough to resist wear. Grooves, called treads, are molded into the outside surface of the tire where it contacts the road. These treads channel water away from the interface between the tire and the road surface.

The part of the tire that is actually resting on the road is called the contact patch. The larger the contact patch, the more grip your scooter has on the road surface. The less inflated a tire is, the larger its contact patch. However, the less inflated a tire is, the more its sidewalls flex, creating heat and wear. So, properly inflating a tire attains a balance between grip and wear. Inflation values molded into tire sidewalls are maximum operating pressures for which each specific tire was designed. Do not inflate your scooter's tires to these levels. To find the proper inflation values, refer to your owner's manual.

Of course, tires that carry a heavier load must be inflated to a higher level than those carrying a lighter load. The tire is the first line of defense in suspension action. Before the shocks or forks are made to compress when your scooter hits a bump, the tire deflects. The more load the tire is carrying in the first place, the more it is deflected at rest. When it hits a bump, it will have less available deflection in its sidewalls to absorb the impact. In extreme cases of under inflation, the tire will deflect to the point at which the rim itself makes contact with the surface over which the tire is rolling. This can result in a jolt if you're lucky, or a bent rim if you're not. And you might or might not lose control of your scooter. Properly inflated tires take expected loads into consideration.

Rims generally come from the factory uniformly round and balanced. Tires, however, have inevitable spots where the rubber is thicker than it is at other spots around the circumference. Therefore, balancing weights must be placed on the rim in order to smooth out the oscillations an out-of-balance wheel assembly will create as it rotates at speed. Once these weights are properly placed, the wheel is good to go and needs no further attention. But every time a tire is replaced, the wheel-balancing procedure must be performed again.

Most scooters today use sealed bearings, in which the bearings, cups, races, and collar that ride on the axle are a single unit, with lubricant sealed inside. They are pressed into the wheel assembly, and maintenance is neither required nor can it be performed. Just press them into the wheel assembly, mount the wheel assembly onto the axle, and ride away. The caveat is that sealed wheel bearings have a limited lifespan and must be periodically replaced.

The contact patch of a scooter's tire is exceedingly small; it's up to you to ensure that what little rubber does come into contact with the road is in the best shape possible.
Foto Factory/Shutterstock.com

PROJECT 18
Remove and Reinstall Rear Wheel with Drum Brake

 Time: 1 hour

 Tools: Wrenches; torque wrench and socket

 Talent: 2

 Cost: None

 Parts: Axle grease

 Benefit: Allows access to drum-brake components; only way to change the tire

1

The exhaust system must be removed before the rear wheel can be removed. Remove the exhaust system (see Project 11, page 78). Also, in order to get enough clearance to remove the rear wheel, the fender might have to be removed first. Remove any fender mounting nuts. *Inset:* Remove the rear fender.

2

Loosen the rear-wheel mounting nut. An impact driver works best for this, but you can do it with a wrench.

3

Remove the rear-wheel mounting nut.

4

Pull the wheel away from the drivebox.

5

While the wheel is off, inspect the condition of the brake drum and brake shoes. The drum should be free of grooves, and the pads should not be worn past the indicator grooves.

6

The rear wheel hub has a spline with teeth that fit into spline teeth on the drive axle. Apply a thin coat of grease to the splines.

8

Reinstall the washer and rear-wheel mounting nut. Screw it in until it is finger tight.

7

To reinstall the rear wheel, align the wheel-hub spline teeth with the drive-axle spline teeth and push the rear wheel onto the drive axle.

9

Tighten the rear-wheel mounting nut to the torque value specified in your owner's or service manual. *Inset:* Reinstall the fender. Reinstall the exhaust system (see Project 11, page 78).

PROJECT 19
Remove and Reinstall Front Wheel

 Time: 1 hour

 Tools: Wrenches; torque wrench and sockets; wood block; wire or coat hanger

 Talent: 2

 Cost: None

 Parts: Axle grease; heat-resistant thread locker

Benefit: Only way to change the tire

1

Put the scooter on its center stand. Most scooters sit with the front wheel resting on the ground when they're on the center stand. If this is the case with your scooter, the front will have to be raised before the front wheel can be removed. This can be accomplished by using the center stand as a fulcrum, then pushing the back wheel down and wedging a block under the front of the belly pan. *Inset:* Since the brake disc is attached to the wheel hub, the brake caliper must be removed in order for the wheel to slide away from the forks after the axle is removed. First, remove the caliper-mounting bolts.

2

Remove the caliper. After the caliper is free, don't just let it hang by the brake hose. Use something to suspend it; wire works well for this job. *Inset:* While the caliper is off, check the condition of the brake pads. This would be a good time to replace them if they're worn past the wear indicator grooves.

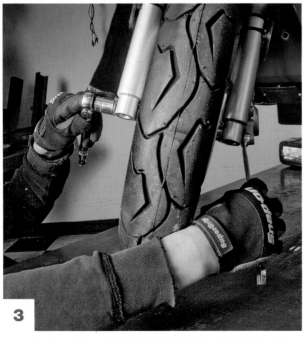

3

Loosen the axle nut. The axle itself is just a long bolt that goes through the wheel hub. You'll need to use a wrench to hold the axle's hex head on one wide of the wheel while you loosen the retaining nut on the other side of the wheel.

4

Remove the axle nut.

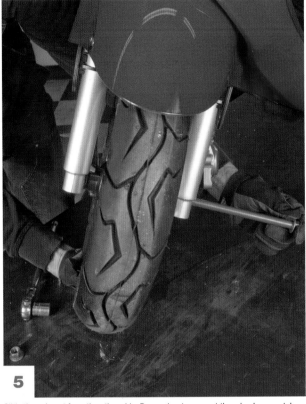

5

Slide the axle out from the other side. Remember to support the wheel as you take the axle out. Be sure not to lose the axle spacer when the wheel comes free of the fork bottoms. Axle spacers are normally on the side of the wheel hub opposite the speedometer drive hub.

6

After the axle is out, pull the wheel away from the scooter. When the speedometer drive hub is clear of the forks, disengage it from the wheel hub. It can hang from the speedometer cable until the wheel is reinstalled.

7

When reinstalling the front wheel, first make sure the axle spacer is in place.

8

The speedometer drive hub has tabs that must fit together into grooves in the wheel hub. Locate the speedometer drive hub tabs.

9

Locate the grooves in the wheel hub.

10

Grease the speedometer drive hub and push it onto the wheel hub.

11

Since the drive hub tabs interlock in the wheel hub grooves, the speedometer drive's natural tendency is to spin as the wheel spins. To keep it in place when your scooter is rolling down the road, the speedometer drive hub has a groove molded into it that fits over a tab molded into the adjacent fork leg. Locate the groove on the speedometer drive hub.

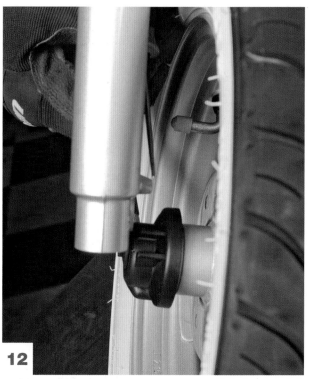

12

Locate the tab molded into the fork leg.

13

Put a light coat of grease onto the axle. Lift the wheel into place and support it. Fit the groove in the speedometer hub over the tab on the fork leg. Reinstall the axle.

14

Reinstall the axle retaining nut. Don't tighten it to the specified torque value yet. You'll need to use a wrench to hold the axle while you tighten the axle retaining nut.

15

Put the brake caliper back into place. Be sure the pads aren't both on one side of the disc.

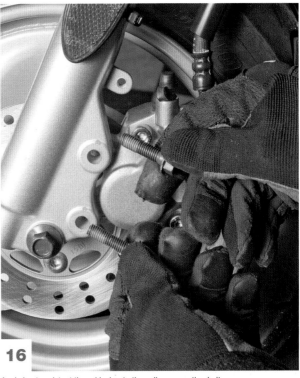

16

Apply heat-resistant thread locker to the caliper-mounting bolts.

17

Install the caliper-mounting bolts.

18

Tighten the caliper bolts to the torque value specified in your owner's or service manual.

19

Tighten the axle retaining nut to the torque value specified in your owner's or service manual. You'll need to use a wrench to hold the axle while you torque the axle retaining nut.

PROJECT 20
Replacing a Tubeless Black Sidewall Tire with a Tubeless White Sidewall Tire

 Time: 2 hours

 Cost: $$

 Tools: Tire-changing machine with bead breaker

 Parts: Tire; lubricant in a spray bottle

Talent: 4

 Benefit: Cool wheels

1

Scooter wheel rims are usually made of relatively thin stamped steel. They bend easily, so be very careful when removing scooter tires. Removing scooter tires with tire irons or spoons is not recommended. It's best to use a tire-changing machine. To remove the black sidewall tire from the rim, first deflate the tire. *Inset:* With the valve cap off, you can see the valve core in the valve stem. Remove the valve core. It simply screws out of the valve stem. You'll need a special wrench; some metal valve caps have valve core–pulling sockets built into them. Remove the valve core and set it aside. It's small and wants to roll around. Don't lose it.

2

Look at one of the inside edges of the tire you're going to mount, and notice how it is built up. This is called the tire's bead. It seats in a groove molded into the outside edge of the rim. Before the tire can be removed, you must first force the tire's bead out of the rim's groove. This is called breaking the bead. It is done by forcing the edge of the tire toward the center of the rim. Start at one point.

3

Work your way around the tire until the bead is completely free of the groove in the rim. Repeat Steps 3 and 4 on the other side of the wheel. The tire should now be completely free of the rim.

4

Mount the wheel onto the tire-changing machine.

5

Spray a lubricant around the bead. A solution of soap and water will work, but specially formulated tire-changing lubricant is also available. Be sure to soak the bead of the tire, since that's what will be sliding over the rim.

6

Pry the outer side of the tire off the top edge of the rim. Start at one point and pull the bead over the rim. This isn't easy and requires a fair amount of force.

7

Begin working your way around the tire, prying the bead over the rim as you go.

8

Once you work your way back to where you started, the top of the tire will be completely free of the rim.

9

Now you have to pry the bottom side of the tire off the rim. Again, start at one point and pull the bead over the top edge of the rim. As it was on the other side, this isn't easy and requires a fair amount of force.

10

Begin working your way around the tire, prying the bead over the edge of the rim.

11

Once you work your way back to where you started, the tire will be completely free of the rim.

12

To install the white sidewall tire, first lubricate the beads. Be sure to lubricate the beads on both sides of the tire. After the solution has been sprayed on, spread it around with your fingers to make sure the whole surface of the bead is covered. Do this on both sides of the tire.

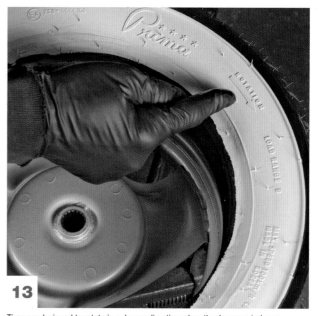

13

Tires are designed to rotate in only one direction when they're mounted on a scooter. Find the directional arrow molded into the sidewall of the tire. The arrow points in the direction the tire will roll when mounted on the scooter. Determine which way the wheel will roll when mounted on the scooter, and be sure the directional arrow on the tire points the same way as you prepare to mount it on the rim.

14 Begin mounting the new white sidewall tire by starting at one point of the bottom bead and forcing it over the top edge of the rim. *Inset:* Work your way around the tire, pushing the bottom bead over the rim.

15 Once you work your way back to where you started, the bottom edge of the tire will be completely in the center of the rim.

16 Now start at one point of the top bead and force it over the top edge of the rim.

17

Work your way around the tire, pushing the bead over the edge of the rim. The last quarter of the way will be the hardest.

18

Once you work your way back to where you started, the whole tire will be completely in the center of the rim.

19

Now you have to seat the bead. Remember how you pushed the bead out of the groove in the rim before you removed the tire? Now you have to force it back in. The easiest way to do this is with compressed air. You can seat the bead with a hand pump, but it's very difficult. Don't reinstall the valve core yet, since a quick burst of air is exactly what you need, and the valve core will only impede the air flowing into the tire. Inflate the tire until the bead seats completely. You'll hear a series of pops as the bead seats its way around the rim. You can see in the photo that this bead has not fully seated yet; the far side has, but the near side hasn't. Be sure the bead is fully set on both sides. Remove the air chuck from the valve stem. The air that is inside the tire will begin to rush out, since the valve core hasn't been reinstalled yet. Let it. Wipe off any excess lubricant.

20

Once all the air has rushed out of the tire, screw the valve core back into the valve stem and inflate the tire to the manufacturer's recommended tire pressure. There's an air-pressure value molded into the sidewall of the tire. This is the maximum pressure the tire will withstand, not the pressure the tire should be under at equilibrium. Do not inflate the tire to the value molded onto the tire's sidewall.

Chapter 12
Brakes

HOW THEY WORK

Newton's first law of motion says that objects in motion tend to stay in motion until acted upon by an external force. In your scooter's case, that force is its brakes. Of course, friction will eventually slow your scooter if you just coast, but for more immediate stopping needs you obviously must apply the brakes.

As with coasting, friction will create the stopping power, but instead of the natural friction of drivetrain components, brakes provide infinitely controllable friction to the wheels. This friction is created either by clamping a caliper onto a disc (disc brakes) or by pushing a shoe outward against a drum (drum brakes). The disc is attached to the wheel hub; the drum is an integral part of the wheel hub. Calipers are made to clamp and shoes are made to push in one of two ways: by using a lever to push hydraulic fluid or by using a lever to pull a cable. Hydraulic brakes can use discs or drums. Cable brakes are usually limited to drum applications.

The levers used to actuate the front and rear brakes of most scooters are on the handlebars. If there's a little reservoir of fluid attached to the lever, you have hydraulic brakes. If the lever is attached to a cable, your scooter has cable-actuated brakes.

STRENGTHS AND WEAKNESSES

Hydraulic brake systems are more reliable, provide more consistent stopping power, and generally require less maintenance than cable-actuated brake systems. The downside is that, when they do need attention, hydraulic brakes can be more intimidating, because they have a lot more parts that seem to work in mysterious ways.

Hydraulic brakes rely on two sets of pistons in cylinders, between which is a hose. The brake lever pushes the first piston (in the master cylinder), which pushes hydraulic brake fluid through the hose, eventually pushing on the second piston (in the slave cylinder, located in the caliper), which in turn pushes the brake pad out, clamping it against the disc. When the brake lever is released, the master cylinder relieves the hydraulic pressure acting on the slave cylinder, and the rotating brake disc pushes the pads back out until they no longer create friction.

As long as there are no leaks, there is sufficient fluid, and there is no air in the system, hydraulic brakes will work dependably. If fluid leaks out or air leaks in, however, the system will fail. Perhaps not all at once—a small fluid leak will eventually deplete the supply in the reservoir and air will enter the system, causing a spongy feel at the lever.

Hydraulic disc brakes are standard fare today, but great big cable-operated drum brakes used to be state of the art.

This is because air compresses much more easily than brake fluid.

When there's no air in the system, the master cylinder piston pushes almost directly against the slave cylinder piston through the brake fluid in the brake line. When air bubbles get into the brake line, instead of using the lever's travel to push the fluid directly from the master cylinder into the slave cylinder, some of the pressure is used up pushing the fluid on one side of the air bubbles into the fluid on the other side of the air bubbles. After enough fluid has leaked out of the system, all the lever travel, thus all the master cylinder piston movement, will be used up compressing air and no pressure will get to the slave cylinder at all. In which case, your brakes will not work at all.

Cable-actuated brakes are far simpler. Between the brake lever on the handlebars and the actuating arm on the drum is a cable. Pull on the brake lever and it pulls on the cable. The cable then pulls on a lever on the drum, which rotates a cam and forces the shoe out against the drum. It's that simple.

The cable can stretch over time, but adjustments can take up the slack—to a certain point. Eventually, every cable that doesn't break gets stretched past the limits of adjustability and must be replaced. Of course, cables can flat out break, but replacing a broken cable is much easier than flushing and bleeding a hydraulic brake system, or worse, rebuilding master cylinders and slave cylinders. Stay on top of cable adjustment, keep the cables lubricated properly, and replace them when they show signs of wear or get stretched past the point of adjustability, and your cable brake system should provide you with reliable stopping power when you need it.

DISC BRAKES

While cable-operated disc brakes exist, scooter applications are rare. Therefore, we'll focus on hydraulic disc brake systems.

The first component in the system is the master cylinder. It consists of a reservoir for brake fluid, a piston to push brake fluid through the brake line, and a lever that pushes the piston. While master cylinder failure is rare, it can occur.

The most common problem is depletion of the supply of brake fluid in the reservoir. As the piston pushes brake fluid through the line, it draws fluid from the reservoir to replace the fluid pushed into the line. If the reservoir level gets too low, air can get drawn into the brake line instead of fluid. If this happens, the whole system will need to be bled.

Since the brake system is a closed system, low fluid levels in the reservoir indicate a leak. Leaks can be from a cracked or cut line, loose connections where the line meets the master cylinder or caliper, worn master or slave cylinders and pistons, or cracks in the master or slave cylinders.

Another potential problem is that the piston or cylinder wall can get scored. This is usually the result of dirt getting into the master cylinder from the reservoir. If the scratches aren't too deep, the piston can be cleaned with emery cloth and the cylinder can be honed. Be careful, though. If too much metal is removed, the piston will become too small for the cylinder. Master cylinder rebuild kits might be available for your scooter.

Over time, the piston and cylinder will become worn though normal use. The rubber gaskets can also become brittle and crack. Again, rebuild kits might be available, as are complete replacement master cylinder assemblies.

Between the master and slave cylinders is the brake line. Your scooter probably uses mesh-reinforced rubber hose, but steel-braided line is also available. When the piston in the master cylinder pushes the brake fluid through the line, the rubber hose expands slightly under the pressure. Steel-braided line resists the pressure of the brake fluid, so more of it is able to act directly on the piston in the slave cylinder. While steel-braided line is commonly used for high-performance applications, rubber brake line will perform dependably under most circumstances.

Both rubber and steel-braided brake line will develop cracks as they age. Rubber brake line can also be cut. Inspect the brake lines periodically, and replace them if they show signs of wear or aging.

At the end of the brake line is the brake caliper. This houses the slave cylinder and the brake pads. The slave cylinder can become worn over time, and the tolerances between the piston and cylinder walls can become sloppy. Also, rubber gaskets can become brittle and crack. In extreme cases of wear, the piston and cylinder walls can become scored from dirt, causing the cylinder to leak. Worse still, the piston can become stuck in the cylinder, preventing it from retracting when the brake lever is released. If this happens, the pads will always apply pressure to the disc, creating excessive heat, wearing out the pads and warping the disc. Rebuild kits and complete replacement components are available.

The slave cylinder piston clamps the brake pads onto the brake disc to provide braking power. Brake pads consist of a steel backing plate with a pad of other material built onto one side. The composition of this material varies. Some pads are designed to be used for a long time; other pads are designed to give better stopping performance. Either way, the material

Hydraulic disc brakes are state of the art today, but they use the same principle as caliper brakes on a bicycle. While bicycle brakes can only exert as much force you apply to the brake lever with your hand, your scooter's hydraulic disc multiplies that force exponentially, providing enough stopping power to lock up a wheel at high speed. When braking with the front wheel, this presents a conundrum: Since the front wheel has more braking potential as weight transfers forward during the stopping or slowing event, it is the more effective of the two when braking. On the other hand, if you apply the front brake too hard, it will lock up and skid—never a good thing. So depend on your front brake, but be careful.
Evgeny Murtola/Shutterstock.com

is designed to disintegrate a little bit each time the brakes are used. That's why so much black dust accumulates around the caliper. It's all the pad material that's worn away from dragging along the disc.

Check your brake pads regularly. If all the pad material wears away and the metal backing plate is clamped onto the disc when the brakes are applied, it will ruin the disc.

As for the disc, it's that steel or cast-iron plate that attaches to the wheel assembly. Discs will wear out over time. Check the width of the disc. If it gets below the minimum thickness listed in your owner's or shop manual, replace the disc. In addition to normal wear, discs can get scored if dirt gets between the pad and the disc when the brakes are applied. This is evident by grooves that get worn into the disc. Worn or grooved discs must be replaced.

DRUM BRAKES

Drum brakes can be operated hydraulically or by cable. Since hydraulic disc and drum brake systems function in essentially the same way, refer to the Disc Brake section of this chapter for information on hydraulic system operation.

As described in the Strengths and Weaknesses section of this chapter, cable drum brakes are simple. At one end of the cable is the brake lever. At the other end is the brake drum. Inside the brake drum are brake shoes and springs. When you pull on the brake lever, it pulls on one end of the cable. As the cable moves through its housing, its other end pulls on a lever that sticks out of the drum, rotating a shaft. Attached to the other end of this shaft is a cam. The brake shoes rest against this cam, held in place by springs. As the shaft rotates, the cam also rotates, forcing the brake shoes outward against the brake drum wall, creating friction. When the brake lever is released and the cam rotates back to its original position, the springs keep the shoes riding along the cam, pulling the shoes back away from the drum wall.

And that's all there is to it. If the cable breaks, replace it. If the shoes wear out, replace them. Keep the brake lever and the shaft at the drum clean and lubricated, occasionally lubricate the cable in the cable housing, adjust the shoes at the recommended intervals, and your cable-operated drum brakes should stop you reliably.

When replacing brake shoes, inspect the inside of the brake drum. If it is scored, it might need to be turned, which is a fancy name for grinding off the surface of the drum until it is smooth again. You'll probably be able to do this with sandpaper, but extreme cases need to go to a machine shop.

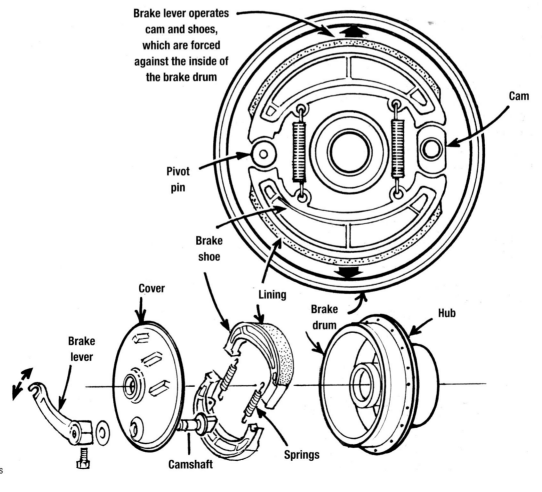

Brake lever operates cam and shoes, which are forced against the inside of the brake drum

Cam

Pivot pin

Brake shoe

Lining

Brake drum

Hub

Cover

Brake lever

Camshaft

Springs

Drum brake parts

PROJECT 21
Remove and Replace Brake Caliper

 Time: 1 hour

 Tools: Wrenches; torque wrench and sockets; drain bottle

 Talent: 2

 Cost: None

 Parts: None

 Benefit: Allows access to brake pads

1

Place a rag over the wheel to protect the wheel and tire from dripping brake fluid. Brake fluid is extremely corrosive. Don't get any on painted surfaces, rubber, chrome—try not to let brake fluid get on anything. If necessary remove any supports that might be holding the brake line in place.

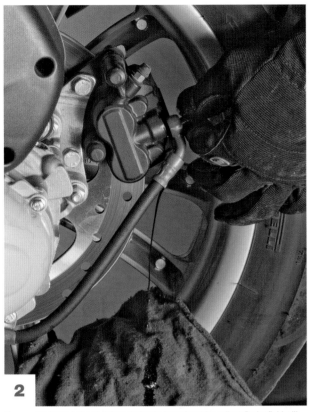

2

Remove the banjo bolt and detach the brake hose from the caliper. Brake fluid will drain as the bolt loosens.

3

Put the open end of the brake line into some kind of drain receptacle to catch any brake fluid that might leak out while you're busy with other duties.

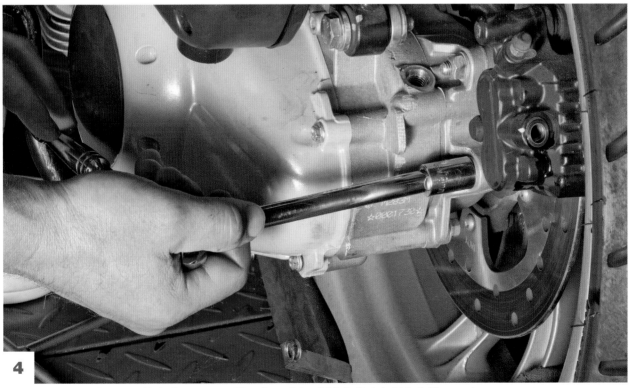

4

Loosen and remove the caliper-retaining bolts. Be sure to support the caliper so it doesn't fall after the last retaining bolt is removed.

5

Remove the caliper.

6

Reinstallation is the reverse of the removal procedure. Be sure to apply thread locker to the caliper-retaining bolts before reinstalling them.

7

Tighten the caliper-retaining bolts and the brake line banjo bolt to their proper torque values (consult your owner's or service manual).

PROJECT 22
Remove and Replace Brake Pads

 Time: 1 hour

 Tools: Allen wrench or drift pin and hammer

⭐ **Talent:** 2

💲 **Cost:** $–$$

Parts: Brake pads

Benefit: A scooter that stops

1

Remove the brake caliper (see Project 21, page 130). Drain the caliper. *Inset:* Remove the brake-pad retaining pins. These usually screw into and out of place, but sometimes they're just friction-fit pins and can be pushed out with a drift and a hammer.

2

Slide the pads out of the caliper. Pay attention to the orientation of the sheet-metal spring that holds the pads in place so you can reinstall it properly.

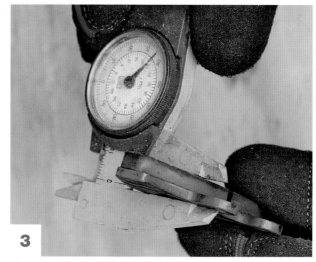

3

Check the condition and thickness of the pads.

4

Replace the pads if necessary. Worn pads will eventually let the metal backing plate make direct contact with the brake disc. If this happens, the disc will get scored and need to be replaced too.

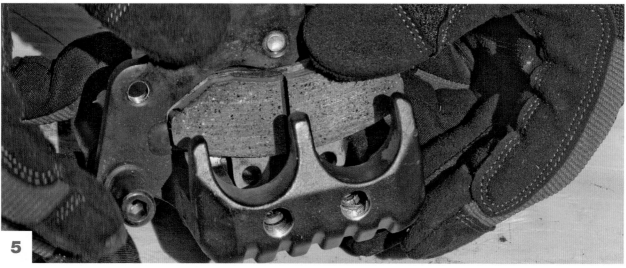

5

Reinstall the brake pads. First install the sheet-metal spring, then put in the pads.

6

Insert the brake-pad retaining pins.

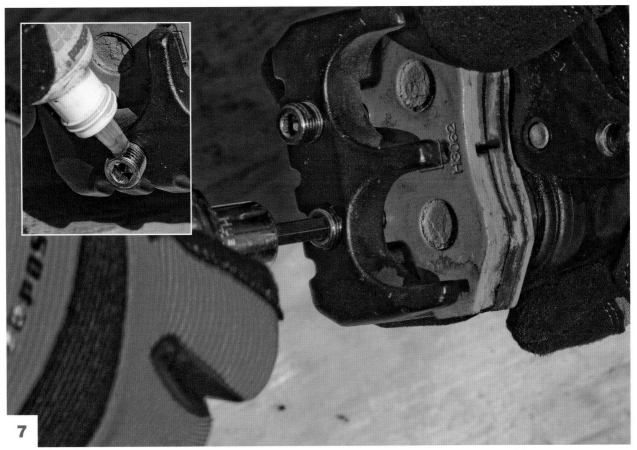

7

Inset: Apply thread locker to the threads. *Main picture:* Tighten the brake-pad retaining pins. Reinstall the brake caliper (see Project 21, page 130).

PROJECT 23
Bleed Brake System

 Time: 1–2 hours

 Tools: Wrenches; torque wrench and sockets; brake-bleeding tool or length of clear plastic hose and drain bottle

 Talent: 4

 Cost: $

 Parts: Brake fluid

 Benefit: Brake levers and pedals that don't feel spongy

BRAKES

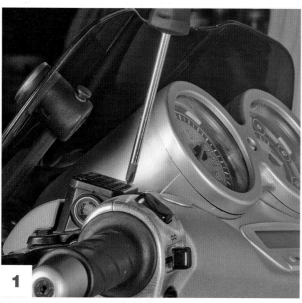

1 Loosen and remove the master-cylinder reservoir-top retaining screws

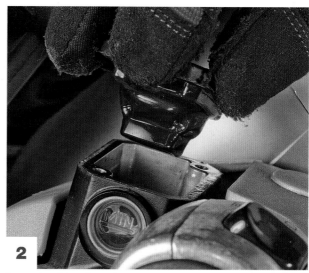

2 Remove the master-cylinder reservoir top. Remove the rubber diaphragm from underneath the aluminum cap. Inspect the diaphragm for damage. Set both the cap and diaphragm aside for cleaning.

Locate the bleeder valve on the caliper. Remove the protective rubber cap. At this point, you need to attach one end of a length of clear, plastic drain hose to the bleeder valve. Put the other end of the drain hose into a container to catch brake fluid as it is expelled from the caliper. The end of the hose should be submerged in a small quantity of brake fluid before beginning the bleeding procedure.

3

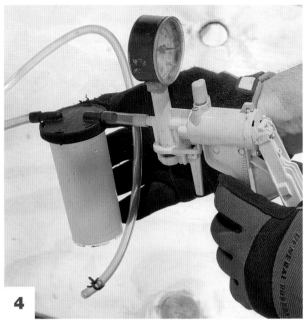

4

Alternatively, you could use a vacuum-assist bleeding tool. This will not only catch the expelled brake fluid, but it will actually pull the brake fluid through the system from the master cylinder reservoir. Attach the open end of the vacuum tool's hose to the brake caliper bleeder valve.

5

If you're using a vacuum-assist bleeding tool, pump it up and open the bleeder valve 1/8 to 1/4 turn. Don't go too far. If you leave it too loose and sloppy, air will leak through the threads and you'll always see bubbles in the draining brake fluid. Just turn the bleeder valve far enough for the fluid to start flowing brake fluid. Also keep in mind that you'll probably be alternately opening and closing the bleeder valve while pumping the brake lever, so the shorter your stroke the more accurately you can time the cycle.

6

Even if you're using a vacuum-assist bleeding tool, it pays to apply the following conventional bleeding methods. This involves squeezing the brake lever firmly but slowly. As pressure is applied to the lever, open the bleeder valve. Keep it open as the lever moves toward the handlebar. Close the bleeder valve before the lever meets the bar. Slowly release the lever.

7 Repeat Step 6 until there are no air bubbles seen in the drain hose, just a healthy stream of brake fluid. If your stream looks like the one in this photo, you're not done yet.

8 **This is important!** Be sure to maintain an adequate level of brake fluid in the master-cylinder reservoir. Cover the area surrounding the reservoir with a rag before adding fluid. Brake fluid is highly corrosive. You want stray drips to go onto the rag, not your scooter.

BRAKES

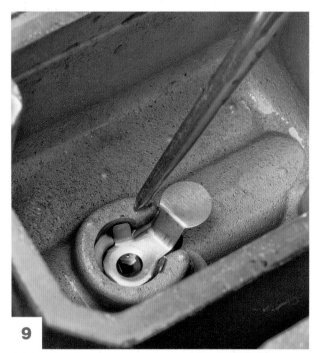

9 If the brake fluid level gets too low, air can be drawn into the system through the reservoir. If this happens, all the fluid between the newly induced air bubble at the reservoir and the bleeder valve will need to be purged in order to suck out the offending air bubble. In other words, you'll be starting this procedure again from scratch.

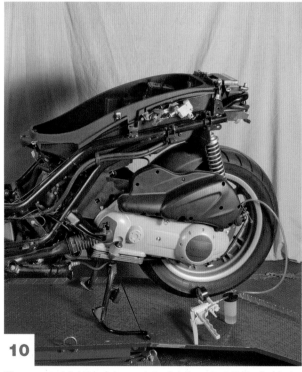

10 When no more air bubbles can be seen in the drain hose, simply tighten the bleeder valve and replace its protective rubber cap, remove the drain hose, and reinstall the master-cylinder reservoir and diaphragm.

Chapter 13
Body Parts

HOW IT WORKS

Just about every scooter is completely encased in body panels. These can be made of fiberglass but most likely are made of plastic. They fit together with interlocking tabs and are held in place by screws. Some of these screws attach one body panel to another, and screw through holes in one panel into metal tabs clipped onto the other. Other screws attach a body panel to the scooter and screw through a hole in the body panel into a threaded hole in the frame.

The front fender is normally a finished body part that stands on its own visually, while the rear fender is usually made of black plastic and hidden by the rear body panels.

The seat either flips up or can be removed entirely. Some latches require a key; others are released by a button or a lever.

Gas and oil tanks are usually hidden by body panels. The tanks are made of plastic and can be located by their filler caps.

Most scooters also have one or more storage compartments, which are usually located under the seat and behind the front panel. They are made of plastic and can be removed. Removing the under-seat storage compartment, for example, allows more unfettered access when working on the engine.

STRENGTHS AND WEAKNESSES

Body panels serve two functions: To protect your scooter's various systems from the elements and to add aerodynamics. Unless they get cracked, body panels usually do a good job of the former. As for the latter, they're successful or they're not so successful, depending on the particular model.

Even if your scooter just falls over in a parking lot, its body panels are bound to suffer some damage, probably just scratches but cracks are possible. If you drop your scooter while riding it, one or more of its body panels will most likely have to be replaced. While scratches can be ignored and hairline cracks can be filled and reinforced, massively broken panels cannot be repaired.

BODY PANELS

Starting up front, your scooter's frame is encased by the front panel. This is the one you see when the scooter is coming directly at you. The panel you see up front when you're sitting at the scooter's controls is the kick panel. This kick panel continues under your feet until it gets to the side panels in the rear. Underneath the scooter is the belly panel. At the rear of the scooter are the side panels. These can be one- or two-piece designs.

Pretty much every scooter is completely encased in body panels. Not every scooter has this many mirrors. Made popular by the Who's rock-and-roll opera, *Quadrophenia*, British scooter riders known as Mods followed a trend in which they tried to see how many mirrors they could fit onto their scooters. Great rear-view visibility, but really expensive if you crash.

Body panels must be removed (and replaced) in a certain order. Some fit over others, some fit under others, some clip together. If you try to take one off when it's still partially covered by or clipped into another, you can break off little (or big) pieces. At best, a broken clip will leave your panel flapping in the wind. At worst, whole bits of panel will disappear, necessitating replacement. Refer to your owner's manual for the correct removal and reinstallation procedures for your scooter.

FENDERS

Your scooter's front fender mainly keeps your scooter from looking like it's been splashing through mud puddles. It's not so much for keeping you dry, since the front panel does that pretty well by itself. The rear fender, however, keeps everything under the side panels from getting sprayed with whatever loose debris (wet or solid) the rear wheel encounters on the road. What's underneath the side panels? Wiring harnesses, electrical components, the engine—in other words, the fender protects most of the working parts of your scooter.

Unless you crash, neither fender is likely to need much attention.

SEAT

The seat either flips up or can be removed entirely. It consists of a metal pan on top of which is foam rubber covered by imitation or real leather. Periodically apply some sort of appropriate protective compound to the seat cover to keep it pliable. If the cover rips, it should be replaced; otherwise the elements will degrade the foam rubber underneath.

GAS AND OIL TANKS

Gas and oil tanks generally don't need to be removed unless they develop leaks and must be replaced. Some service procedures require that they be removed in order to gain access to other components. If you need to remove a tank, remember to drain it first.

STORAGE COMPARTMENTS

The underseat storage bin can be removed to gain access to the engine. Follow the steps in your owner's or service manual. Occasionally, other components are mounted to the storage bin and must first be removed.

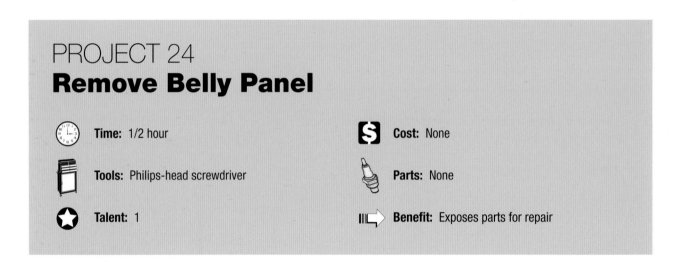

PROJECT 24
Remove Belly Panel

Time: 1/2 hour

Tools: Philips-head screwdriver

Talent: 1

Cost: None

Parts: None

Benefit: Exposes parts for repair

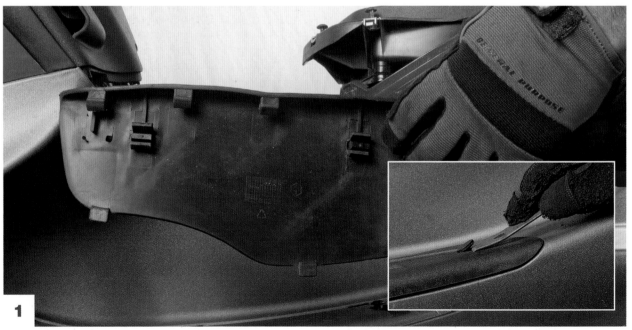

1

First, remove the rear footpeg (see Project 32, page 150). Next, remove the rubber footpad. It's held in place around the side by tabs molded into the edge of the rubber pad that fit into holes in the belly panel). In the middle, the pad is held in place by rubber retaining plugs that fit through holes in the pad and the belly panel. *Inset:* Pry out the retaining plugs.

2

Remember that the retaining tabs go all the way around the pad. Starting with the tabs on the outside edge, slide the tabs out of their holes.

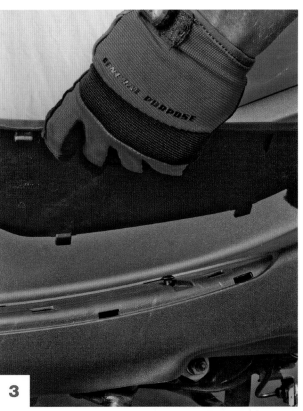

3

After all the outside-edge tabs are pulled out, pry up the middle, then work the inside tabs out of their holes. Lift the pad off the belly panel.

4

Remove the large retaining screws.

5

Remove the small retaining screws. Lift off the belly panel.

PROJECT 25
Remove Floor Panel

 Time: 1/2 hour

 Tools: Philips-head screwdriver

 Talent: 1

 Cost: None

 Parts: None

 Benefit: Exposes parts for repair

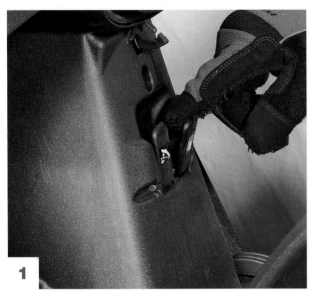

1 Open the gas cap access panel, if there is one.

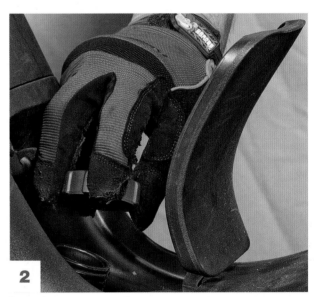

2 Remove the gas cap.

3 Locate and remove the floor-panel retaining screws.

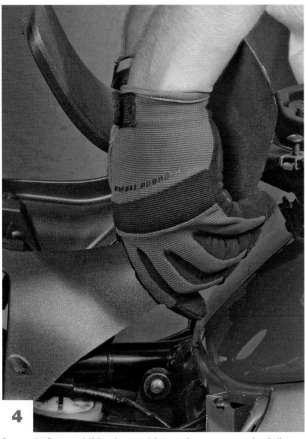

4 Remove the floor panel. If there's a remotely opened gas-cap access door in the panel, you'll have to disconnect the cable.

5 Slide the gas-cap access-door cable end out of the clip.

6 Remove the cable.

7 Replace the gas cap.

PROJECT 26
Remove Side Panel

 Time: 1/2 hour

 Cost: None

Tools: Philips-head screwdriver

Parts: None

 Talent: 1

Benefit: Exposes parts for repair

1

If your scooter has a one-piece side panel assembly, the retaining screws will have to be removed from both sides and the rear before the assembly can be removed. If your scooter has a two-piece side panel assembly, the two pieces will overlap at the front and the rear, where they will both be connected to the frame with retaining screws. Determine which side overlaps the other, and remove it first. Start by removing the large retaining screws.

2

Remove the small retaining screws.

3

Lift off the panel. There may be retaining tabs molded into the body panel, so do this step carefully. The tabs fit through holes in other body panels. If your scooter has a two-piece side panel assembly, there will definitely be tabs where the two panels connect at the front and the rear. You might need to slide the panel to disengage these clips before pulling the panel away from the scooter.

PROJECT 27
Remove Rear Wheel Fender/Mudguard

 Time: 1/2 hour

 Tools: Philips-head screwdriver; wrenches

⭐ **Talent:** 1

 Cost: None

 Parts: None

 Benefit: Exposes rear wheel for removal

1 If your scooter's turn-signal mounts are molded into the rear mudguard, you'll need to disconnect the rear turn-signal electrical connections. You'll also need to disconnect the taillight electrical connections. First, label each receptacle to help you remember which connects to what during reassembly.

2 Thread the turn-signal wires through any holes they might go through.

3 Remove the side mudguard retaining screws.

4 Remove the main retaining screws that hold the top of the mudguard.

5 Lift off the mudguard.

PROJECT 28
Remove Seat

 Time: 1/2 hour

 Tools: Philips-head screwdriver

 Talent: 1

 Cost: None

 Parts: None

 Benefit: Exposes parts for repair

1

Unlatch the seat.

2

Lift the seat into the open position.

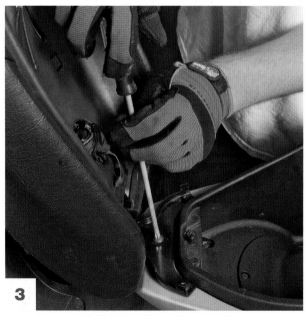

3

Remove the screws that attach the seat hinge to the scooter's frame.

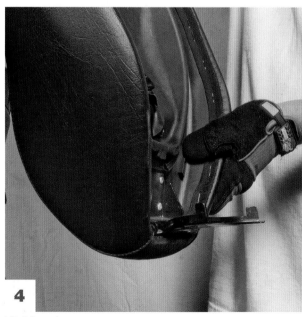

4

Lift off the seat.

PROJECT 29
Remove Under-Seat Storage Bin

 Time: 1/2 hour

 Tools: Philips-head screwdriver

 Talent: 1

Cost: None

Parts: None

Benefit: Exposes parts for repair

1

Remove the seat (see Project 28, page 146) and any other components that are attached to the under-seat storage bin in any way.

2

If there's a mat at the bottom of the storage area, remove it. *Inset:* Remove the battery-compartment cover and disconnect the battery. Disconnect the negative cable first, then the positive cable. Remove the battery.

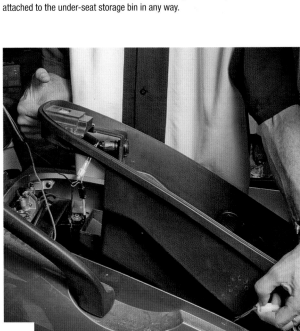

3

Disconnect any wires or hoses that might run through the bin itself.

4

Remove under-seat storage bin retaining screws and lift bin up and out of scooter.

PROJECT 30
Remove Grab Handle

Time: 1/2 hour

Tools: Wrenches

Talent: 1

Cost: None

Parts: None

Benefit: Exposes parts for repair

1 Remove the battery cover if necessary (see Project 31, page 149). If you can't see the grab-handle mounting screws, they might be hidden beneath a plastic cover. Pry loose the plastic cover.

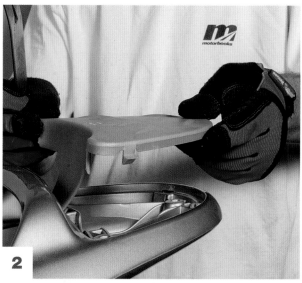

2 Remove the plastic cover to expose the grab-handle retaining screws.

3 Remove the grab-handle mounting screws.

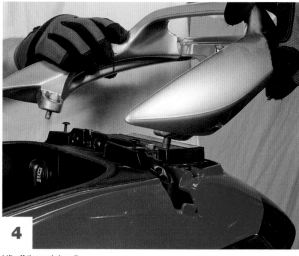

4 Lift off the grab handle.

PROJECT 31
Remove Battery Cover

 Time: 1/2 hour

 Tools: Philips-head screwdriver

⭐ **Talent:** 1

$ **Cost:** None

Parts: None

▮▮▷ **Benefit:** Exposes parts for repair

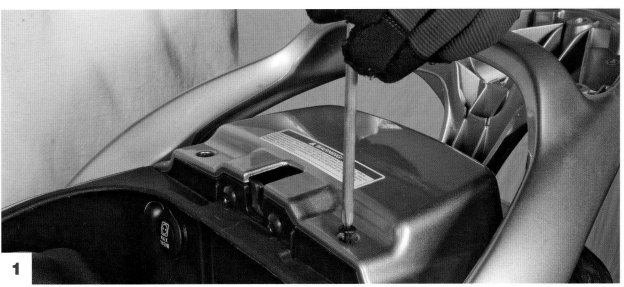

1

Remove the battery-cover retaining screws.

2

There are retaining tabs molded into the battery cover to help hold it in place. Slide the cover back to disengage these tabs. Lift the cover off to expose the battery.

149

PROJECT 32
Remove Rear Footrest

 Time: 1/2 hour

 Tools: Philips-head screwdriver

 Talent: 1

 Cost: None

 Parts: None

 Benefit: Exposes parts for repair

1

Remove the retaining screw.

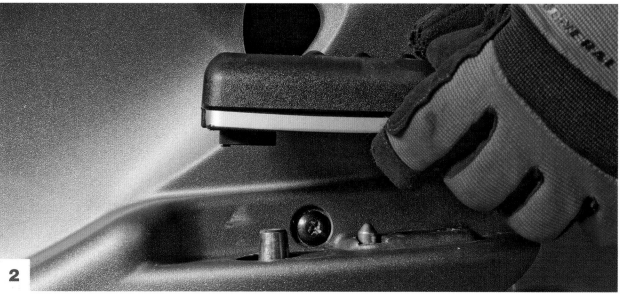

2

Lift off the footrest.

PROJECT 33
Remove Side Panel Trim Pieces

 Time: 1/2 hour

Tools: Philips-head screwdriver

 Talent: 1

Cost: None

Parts: None

Benefit: Exposes parts for repair

1 Remove the retaining screws.

2 There are retaining tabs molded into the trim piece to help hold it in place.

3 Holding the nuts in back with a wrench, remove the retaining screws from the front. The tab in front will act as a hinge when removing the panel. Be careful not to break it off. Slide the back of the panel out and then slide the whole panel back to release the retaining clips. Remove the panel. rench.

Chapter 14
Electrical System (Chassis and Body)

As scooter bodies became more sophisticated, their electrical systems became more complex. Nowadays, Gold Wings aren't the only two-wheelers with travel trunks.

HOW IT WORKS

The charging system is the root of the electrical system. The alternator creates electrical energy, and the battery stores it. The battery also serves as the power source for your scooter's electrical system. Everything runs through the battery. It provides power to the starter motor when you turn the key or push the starter button; it sends electricity to the turn signals when you move the turn-signal switch. It is essential that the battery be in good working order.

WIRING HARNESS

Your scooter's wiring harness is akin to your own wiring harness, your spinal cord. Both are a bundle of wires that run along the skeleton—in your case your spine, in your scooter's case, its frame.

Your scooter's wiring harness is made up of electrical wire that carries electrical current to all of its electrical components, from headlights to the starter motor. While wires don't generally just go bad, it can happen. More likely, however, if a wire in the wiring harness is bad, it's due to external damage. It's possible to replace wires in the wiring harness, but it's labor intensive. On the other hand, it might well be cheaper than putting in a whole new harness.

FUSES

Your scooter's electrical system is protected by fuses. Each circuit has a fuse, which will burn through, or blow, if excess current is demanded. Excess current is demanded if there is a fault, such as a short circuit or faulty component. If such a situation exists, the fuse is designed to blow before more serious damage can occur.

The first thing to check in a malfunction that might involve the electrical system is the attendant fuse. If your headlights don't work, check the fuse in that circuit. If your turn signals don't work, check the fuse in that system. Etcetera.

HANDLEBAR SWITCHES

Many electrical system components are controlled by handlebar switches. While failure is rare, handlebar switches can malfunction. If your scooter's turn signals don't work or the horn doesn't blow or the starter motor doesn't engage, and component and wiring faults have been eliminated, the problem might well lie in the handlebar switch. These switches can be replaced quite easily.

One switch that can cause problems is the kill switch. If the starter doesn't work or your scooter cuts out intermittently, check the kill switch. Accidentally bumping the kill switch and moving it to the "off" position is probably the number one reason a scooter won't start.

LIGHTS

The most common electrical problem is burned out light bulbs. If your scooter's headlight doesn't come on, or one of the turn signals doesn't work, or the license plate isn't illuminated, or the oil light doesn't come on, the first thing to check is the bulb. Then check the fuse. If all else fails, start checking the wiring from the bulb socket back to the switches. Eventually you will find the problem.

GAUGES AND WARNING LIGHTS

Most likely the fuel gauge is the only electrically operated gauge on your scooter. Speedometers are usually driven by a cable, and scooters don't usually have tachometers. If the fuel gauge doesn't work, first check the fuse, then go backward through the system to the sensor in the tank.

Warning lights should come on when the ignition is first switched on. If a warning light doesn't come on when the key is turned one, the bulb is probably burned out. If not, check the bulb socket and wiring. The oil warning light also has a diode in the circuit, which might be faulty.

The relatively simple electrical system found in the average scooter is the system most likely to fail. *Marijus Seskauskas/Shutterstock.com*

PROJECT 34
Replace Taillight or Brake Light Bulb

 Time: 1/4 hour

 Tools: None

 Talent: 1

 Cost: $

 Parts: Taillight/brake-light bulb

 Benefit: Avoid rearend collisions

1 Remove the taillight/brake-light assembly (see Project 36, page 156). Remove the bulb socket from the rear of the assembly.

2 With the socket free of the taillight/brake-light assembly, remove the bulb by grasping it, pushing it in, then turning it clockwise until it stops. Now pull it straight out of the socket.

3 To install the new bulb, align the posts on the side with the grooves in the socket, insert the new bulb into the socket, push the bulb all the way in, then turn it counterclockwise until it seats. Replace the taillight/brake-light assembly.

PROJECT 35
Replace Turn-Signal Bulb

 Time: 1/4 hour

 Cost: $

 Tools: Philips-head screwdriver

 Parts: Turn-signal bulb

 Talent: 1

Benefit: Avoid collisions

1

Remove the turn-signal lens retaining screw.

2

Remove the turn-signal lens. The side opposite the retaining screw is held in place by a tab molded into the lens. After removing the retaining screw, the lens should pivot on the tab, then slide out.

3

Remove the inner diffuser socket from the turn-signal body.

4

Grasping the bulb and the diffuser socket assembly, push the bulb into the socket slightly and twist it clockwise until it stops. Remove the bulb by pulling it straight out of the socket. Install the new bulb by aligning the posts on the side of the bulb with the grooves in the socket and pushing the new bulb into the socket as far as it can go, then twist the bulb counterclockwise until it seats.

5

When reinstalling the diffuser, make sure that the cutaway on the side lines up with the tab in the turn-signal body. Similarly, when reinstalling the turn-signal lens, make sure the tab on the lens lines up with the groove in the turn-signal body.

PROJECT 36
Remove Taillight Assembly

Time: 1/2 hour

Tools: Philips-head screwdriver

Talent: 1

Cost: None

Parts: None

Benefit: Allows access to bulbs

ELECTRICAL SYSTEM (CHASSIS AND BODY)

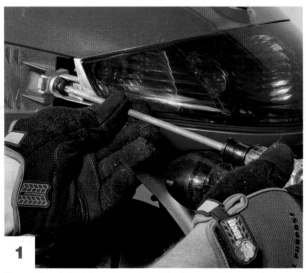

1

Remove the main retaining screws.

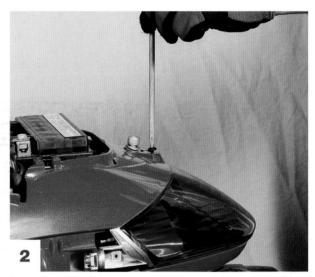

2

Remove the small retaining screws.

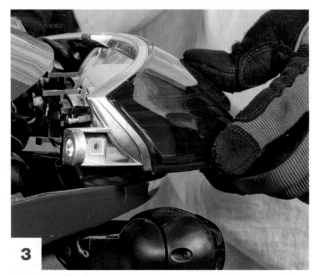

3

Slide out the taillight/brake-light assembly.

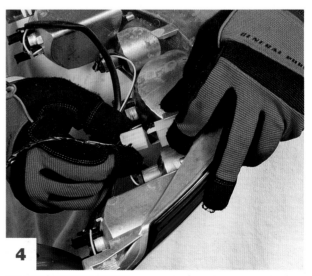

4

Disconnect the electrical junction.

PROJECT 37
Remove Rear Turn-Signal Assembly

 Time: 1/2 hour

 Tools: Wrenches; Philips-head screwdriver

 Talent: 1

 Cost: None

 Parts: None

 Benefit: Allows removal of rear mudguard

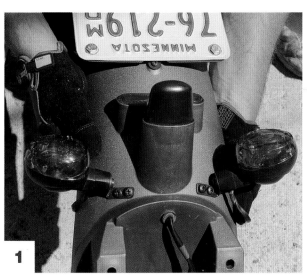

1 Locate the retaining screws on the outer face of the mudguard.

2 Locate the retaining-screw nuts on the inner face of the mudguard.

3 Holding the nuts in back with a wrench, remove the retaining screws from the front.

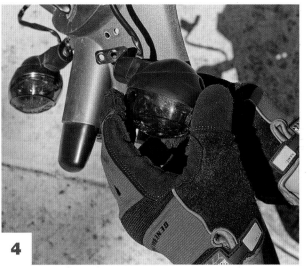

4 Lift off the turn-signal assembly.

ELECTRICAL SYSTEM (CHASSIS AND BODY)

Index

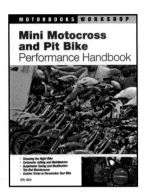    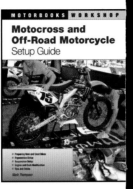